"Some people tell stories in a way that refreshes the soul and leaves you with a deeper sense of contentment and joy. John is this kind of storyteller. The stories are sincere, the journey through them is fascinating, and the focus is clearly Jesus. As I read John's stories, I was privileged to experience a quiet refreshment of the soul. I hope you do too!

- JEREMY MILLER
President of Rosedale Bible College (formerly John's pastor)

D1712059

"Over two million men and women are caged like cattle in the cold and often unjust American prison system. It's a jungle of despair and darkness. Prison rarely, if ever, rehabilitates. It only hardens the hearts of those who have been wounded and confined. There is only one thing that can bring even a shred of hope into such a hopeless world: The gospel of Jesus Christ.

John Schmid has been entering the sinister world of prison and sharing the love and hope of the gospel with thousands of prisoners over the course of many decades. Here are the stories of his journey to bring hope and healing and life to the lost and forgotten people in the world's most harsh and desolate places."

- IRA WAGLER

"Combos are common on a restaurant menu, but John Schmid provides the real deal through his authentic storyteller/singer Combo–nation! Be it in a living room, concert hall, cruise ship, or prison chapel, my long-time friend John Schmid (45 years) is the most versatile Christian communicator I've ever known. Readers of this book will have their vision enlarged and receive hope to fulfill unrealized dreams."

— NELSON COBLENTZ
Founder/Executive Director, Gospel Express Ministries

"John Schmid is quite a treasure as a minstrel and Christian folk philosopher. On these pages, you can travel with him around his northeastern Ohio community and the rest of the world. You'll have prison visits, Central American mission trips, benefit concerts, and churches—all in colorful English, Spanish, and even Pennsylvania Dutch."

— LEVI MILLER
Missionary (Venezuela); Author (Ben's Wayne, Our People, & others)
Director, Herald Press; Director, Mennonite Historical Committee; Minister;
All around good guy...

JOHN SCHMID

SHOWING UP

I WAS IN PRISON AND YOU VISITED ME

1995 - 2005

BOOK TWO

JPV PRESS

Unless otherwise noted, Scripture is from the Holy Bible, King James Version, Public Domain.

Printed in the United States of America

First Printing, 2018

ISBN 978-1-946389-09-1

JPV ❧ PRESS
2106 Main Street / PO Box 201
Winesburg, OH 44690

www.jpvpress.com

DEDICATION

I DEDICATE THIS BOOK TO BUSINESSMAN AND FELLOW
CHURCH MEMBER LEVI TROYER, WHO SAID, "IF YOU GO
INTO PRISON MINISTRY, I'LL SUPPORT YOU." IT WAS
1989 AND I HAD JUST RESIGNED AS YOUTH PASTOR OF
BERLIN MENNONITE CHURCH. I DIDN'T GO INTO PRISON
MINISTRY, BUT HE AND HIS WIFE, LILLIS, SUPPORTED
ME ANYWAY... AND WOULDN'T YOU KNOW... WITHIN 9
MONTHS I WAS DOING PRISON MINISTRY! HIS ENCOURAGE-
MENT WAS JUST WHAT I NEEDED TO START COMMON GROUND
MINISTRIES. THIRTY YEARS AND HUNDREDS OF PRISONS
LATER, LEVI & LILLIS ARE STILL SUPPORTING AND EN-
COURAGING LYDIA AND ME. HOW MANY PRISONERS (AND
OTHER FOLKS) MAY BE IN HEAVEN BECAUSE OF LEVI'S
ENCOURAGING WORD?

OTHER TITLES BY JOHN SCHMID

Encounters
In and Out of Prison with John Schmid
(sequal to Showing Up)

TABLE OF CONTENTS

1997

1998

2004

2005

PREFACE

Ben Franklin said, "If you want to be remembered, do something worth writing about or write something worth reading." It's not so much that I want to be remembered (although I do), but I want my life to count; to make an impact. And I want my children and grandchildren to have a little insight into my life, which will be part of their heritage. How I wish my dad and his dad, and his granddad... would have written down some of their history. Much of my heritage is lost because no one wrote it down.

At a breakfast meeting last week, I tried to convince my friend, Ron Troyer, to write his life story. It would be a thriller. He himself sent me this quote: "An untold story is like a buried treasure that nobody finds."

ACKNOWLEDGMENTS

And having quoted Ron Troyer above, I asked JPV Press to allow me to put these Acknowledgements on the same page so I can say thank you to Marlin Miller, Sue Wengerd, Phil Barkman, Isaac Hershberger... and all the staff at JPV Press for pressuring me to dig up these "treasures." I have wanted to put these stories in writing for 20 years, and Marlin's enthusiasm, persistence and belief in me convinced me to finally uncover these untold stories. So many authors say, "I couldn't have done it without you..." In my case, I WOULDN'T have done it without you! Thank you, thank you!

And thank you, Phil Barkman and Sue Wengerd, for your editing and publishing skills.

JESUS AND THE SYSTEM

I couldn't agree more with the words of Chuck Colson. In a culture that is in total confusion as it gets farther and farther from God and His principles, the only stable anchor we have is Jesus Christ.

> Prisons don't work. They are the most expensive failure of our Western government. There is only one possible hope in the prison system... that is the men and women who take the Good News of Jesus Christ so that lives can be transformed inside those rotten, lousy concrete holes, and they can find new life in Christ and be redeemed, and

come out as productive, law-abiding citizens. There is no other hope... I had to go to prison because I had to be in prison in order for God to use me to start this movement. I shudder to think where I'd be if I had not gone to prison.

– CHUCK COLSON
accepting the Templeton Prize for *All Those in Prison,* July 1993

Right now it is illegal to post the Ten Commandments in our schools, and yet President Clinton wants to hire 50,000 more policemen to enforce those very commandments: arrest those who kill, those who steal, etc. It used to be said that "ignorance of the law is no excuse." We are in such confusion that "ignorance of the law" is enforced in schools.

In a confusing world, as well as a confusing corrections system, Jesus Christ brings stability and purpose to a person's life. "I'm at peace," were the words of John, an inmate at London Correctional Institute. "My wife has left me, and for good reason, the way I treated her. I'm here in prison, locked up, but for the first time in my life, I'm at total peace with God. He has forgiven me, and I feel clean since I got right with Jesus Christ. I feel great."

MAY
We went to five prisons in May. At Warren Correctional we went into protective custody. This is an isolated unit for prisoners who are in danger for one reason or another. At the first unit, we went in and sang and shared from the Word and then went from cell to cell, talking with the men. They were receptive and appreciative, but no one made any commitments.

In the other unit, we sang, and it seemed that no one was even paying attention. Knowing that the Word will not return void, we figured we were just entertaining angels. I stopped singing, and we walked around the room to talk to the men. Two men were playing cards and had not once looked up. I stopped at their table and said, "Hello." They still did not look up. "Hello." There was an awkward pause, and then one of them said, as he picked a card from his hand and flipped it down, "Why did you quit?" He still did not look up. "Because I thought that no one was listening," I said. "Oh no! We were listening! We were just saying how good it sounded." One of them almost looked up, but not quite, and for about ten minutes we talked as they continued playing cards. I walked away realizing that God's Word is heard, even if it seems that there is no response. Now it's up to the Holy Spirit to bring the increase.

June - 1994

A DIVINE APPOINTMENT

"I don't even know where my children are."

That was the statement of the female prisoner—we'll call her Sue—to prison volunteer Brenda Duvendeck, who was part of the Bill Glass Prison Weekend of Champions in northwest Ohio on July 29.

"I think they're in a foster home somewhere."

"I used to keep foster children," said Brenda.

Sue asked her, "Did you ever keep Mark, Linda, and Desiree?"

"Yes! Yes I did!" cried Brenda. "They were at my house several weekends! I have their picture on my refrigerator!"

"Oh, could I see it?" begged Sue. "I don't have any pictures of them."

The next morning Brenda brought the picture from her refrigerator. She showed it to me as we entered the prison. The happy looking children were sitting in Brenda's front yard after a boating trip to Lake Erie. She couldn't wait to show Sue. She handed the picture through the bars, and Sue burst into tears.

"Oh, my children, my children!" She hadn't seen them in six years.

Coincidence? I don't think so. What are the chances of any of the counselors being foster parents and then meeting up with the mother of the very children who had been in her home? It was a divine appointment.

This heartbreaking situation is the norm rather than the exception in our prison system. Broken lives, ruined homes, shattered dreams, hopeless futures—the very thing that our Saviour came to remedy. "I came that they might have life and have it abundantly" (John 10:10 ESV) . For most prisoners, their only hope is Jesus. Actually, for all of us, our only hope is Jesus; we just don't realize it as clearly as Sue and the rest of the inmates do.

I haven't heard the rest of the story on Sue, but I have Brenda's phone number, and I am anxious and excited to see how God is going to restore this family. Pray for Sue.

And what a privilege it was to be a part of the Bill Glass Prison Ministry! I was invited by Jack Murphy to go with him on this weekend and do the singing before he spoke. In five different prisons we did fifteen different performances. I would sing, and when Jack got up to speak and give his testimony of twenty-one years in prison, I would leave and go to the next section of the prison. I would sing until Jack showed up, and then I would take off again to another section and start the program.

On Saturday we did this eight different times! And while we were doing our thing, eight other well-known athletes and world record holders were doing the same thing in other prisons while the several hundred volunteers remained in the prisons to talk and answer questions and lead prisoners—and guards—to Christ. I have not heard the final count, but several hundred decisions for Christ were recorded during the weekend!

LITTLE EDEN
The third week of July was family camp at Little Eden Camp in Onekama, MI. I was the resource person (the new word for speaker), and my responsibilities were a half hour devotional every morning and a program every evening. Even though I spoke twelve times during the week, it proved to be a very relaxing time for my family and me. There was swimming, biking, visiting, loafing, and making new friends, in addition to the spiritual input. Christ was lifted up, and so were we.

August - 1994

FIVE YEARS OF MINISTRY

We officially began as Common Ground Ministries on January 1, 1990. Believe it or not, we are beginning our sixth year of singing and proclaiming Christ in prisons, churches, secular events, and wherever we are invited. We have been in hundreds of prisons in many states and seen prisoners come to Jesus on a consistent basis. Deeper commitments have been made at camps. One of our volunteers is now a prison chaplain in Florida, and another is studying for the ministry. God has also worked in the lives of several others through our short-term mission work trips. One former short-termer is in school studying nursing to work overseas, and another is studying in preparation to serve in Mongolia where her husband worked for a year. I asked these two if the short-term trip had any influence on what they are doing now. They both responded, "A profound influence!"

January - 1995

A LIFE CHANGED

Sid has been in prison for sixteen years for stealing a pickup truck when he was seventeen years old. He actually got three years for the pickup theft. All the rest of the years he acquired while in prison: an escape attempt; a prison riot; striking a guard. Grand total: thirty years. A seventeen-year-old boy steals a truck. The Corrections system begins to correct this wayward youth. Result: thirty years and $510,000 tax dollars later, this teenager, now forty-six years old, is released to live a productive life in society.

Surprisingly, as I talked to Sid during the We Care prison revivals in the Alabama prisons, he showed very little of the bitterness and resentment that usually accompanies imprisonment. "I know I deserve what I got."

Sid came to chapel that night. He sat off to the side. At the invitation, no one responded, which is unusual for a prison service. As I was tearing down the sound equipment, I asked Sid how he liked the service.

"I probably should have stood up at the invitation."

"Why didn't you?" I asked.

"I don't know," was his simple answer.

"Would you like to now?"

"Yes, I would."

The chaplain and I talked and prayed with Sid in the empty chapel and led him into a saving knowledge of Jesus Christ. Our system can keep these young rebels off the streets until they are experienced, hardened men, but only Jesus Christ can change a man from the inside. Pray for Sid, that the Lord will restore the years that the locusts have eaten.

Every year, We Care Prison Ministries, under the direction of Phil Weber, has prison revivals in the Atmore, Troy, and Montgomery areas of Alabama. This year, 250 volunteers from all over the country came to wander through the prison all day and talk and invite men to chapel in the evening.

February - 1995

LA CRUZ, GUANACASTE, COSTA RICA

How can I sum up the twelfth short-term work team that we have taken to Latin America? GREAT! There were twenty-nine of us at the Cleveland Airport on February 24, excited, scared, not sure what to expect. There were two teams in that twenty-nine; one team went to Valle Verde for the fourth year in a row, and I went with fifteen of us to La Cruz, a border town just five miles south of Nicaragua.

For five days we mixed cement, laid block, bent steel, worked, laughed, and prayed. At the workweek's end on Friday, we had the walls up on a pastor's house. It still needs the crown beam, a poured layer of cement around the top that ties walls together in this earthquake-ridden country, and then they will be ready for trusses and roof.

Four of the evenings after work we held evangelistic meetings in the town of La Cruz. Pastor Francisco wanted to use the unusual event of gringos building a house to attract curious villagers to a Billy Graham film, along with an invitation to follow Christ. The first two nights were outside in the streets, and then we went to the church because of the high winds that constantly blew in this northwest corner of Costa Rica.

Saturday was a day with the host families—we stayed in Costa Rican homes—and then on to Arenal Volcano where we met up with Harold Troyer's team from Valle Verde for R&R&D (rest, relaxation, and debrief). Arenal is an active volcano with red-hot lava continuously flowing down the side of its 3,000-foot cone, an awesome sight at night! What a beautiful setting to rest, reflect on what God has done in our lives after this life-changing week, and pray for Him to bring to completion the work He has begun in us.

On March 8, twenty-nine tired, happy missionaries arrived at Cleveland airport. We praise the Lord for the privilege to be able to serve Him in this manner, for a safe trip, and for the relationships He formed among us on the team and with the wonderful Christians in Costa Rica.

Who went? Here is the list in case you are inclined to know: Marv & Neoma, Hartville; Lavern & Marilyn Wagler, Hartville; Troy & Karen Schrock, Berlin; Francis & May Smucker,

Smithville; John & Adam Schmid, Berlin; Alex Beattie, Hesston; Carol Hochstetler & Linda Troyer, Gospel Haven; Betty Miller, East Union; Marneta Beachy, Maranatha; Harold & Debbie Troyer, Rich & Elaine Troyer, Brandon Leatherman, Joanne Miller, Ina Miller, Amy Raber & Myron Hershberger, Grace Mennonite; Kara Yoder, Bethany; Sandra Mast, United Dayspring; Art, Matthew, & Mark Hamsher, Walnut Creek.

March - 1995

FATHER/SON

If you have heard me speak or sing in the last six months, it is possible that I mentioned something about father/son relations. One reason this is on my heart is the age of my son Adam and the terrible statistics of how many prisoners hate their father! As I speak of this in churches, concerts, and prisons, I am made aware that even among Christians there are unresolved hurts and bitterness towards fathers. I am more and more thankful every day for the good home I was born into, and I want to pass on to my children the unconditional love that my dad and mom had for me.

I said all that to say this: At a father/son banquet recently, Adam and I sang some songs together, and I spoke on the importance of a good father/son relationship. At the conclusion of the fun/serious program, I turned it back to the pastor, he felt led to give an invitation, and three young boys and two fathers gave their hearts to Jesus! PTL! They want to be better fathers and sons. The last sentence in the Old Testaments says that before that great and terrible day of the Lord, "And he shall turn the heart of the fathers to the children, and the heart of the children to their fathers, lest I come and smite the earth with a curse" (Malachi 4:6). Could it be that we are approaching the end times and God is fulfilling that prophecy?

P.S. Speaking of father/son: Ten-year-old Adam recently passed the FCC exam to become an amateur radio operator! He is known on the air as KB8YRU. I think I (KD8NT) was more excited than he was. Lydia (KA8UTR) took it all in stride.

April - 1995

BANQUETS!

"This was the best banquet yet!"

Those are the exact words of several of the guests who came to our Common Ground Ministries Spring Banquet. This banquet was different in that we did not seek out a well-known speaker, but instead asked several local folks who have been participants with us in ministry to speak.

Marv Troyer from Hartville talked about his short-term mission experience; Ken Wengerd shared how God used prison ministry to call him into full-time ministry; and David Greer, an ex-convict who just happened to be at the banquet, stood and told how outside ministries can help an inmate. Betty Martin, who shared what it's like to be a parent of someone who's in prison, gave the most heart-rending and revealing talk. All of us got a new perspective on the justice system, and as happened to Ken Wengerd, the men changed from being prisoners to being people: somebody's son, somebody's daddy, somebody's husband. Betty brought that into focus for us in a powerful way.

God has blessed Common Ground Ministries with some great banquets: Jack Murphy, Jim Newsome, Bobby Richardson, and Chaplain Ray—great men with great, encouraging messages. But this local banquet was so good that we're going to begin making our Spring banquets local, and in the Fall we'll invite a well-known speaker. Thanks to all of you who help to make our ministry possible.

LANCASTER CORRECTIONAL
There was a full chapel at Lancaster Correctional on Saturday, April 19, 1995. The chaplain's assistant likes my cassette, so he did some advertising for us. We had a great service, and at the invitation, six men committed their lives to Jesus for the first time! Twelve others recommitted their lives, along with many requests for prayer for family members and other needs. This is the prison where Eric Bache is. He is the boy who ran over ten Amish children two years ago, killing five of them. He sat on the front bench. Chaplain Pursley says that he is genuinely following Jesus. This might be a good time to pray for the Troyer, Kurtz, and Weaver families who lost their precious children.

May - 1995

BIBLE MEMORY CAMP

After working at Bible Memory Camp at Camp Luz and Camp Buckeye for five years, our schedule got so full of prisons that we were not able to be a part of their program in Ohio for the last two years. So at their invitation, we went to Bible Memory Camp at Camp Christian in Chouteau, OK. I was the Bible teacher for two camps: the high school/junior-high weekend, and the second to sixth grader's week. Although I spoke two times a day and had other responsibilities, it was a very refreshing time. Here's why: Lydia and the children were right there at the camp with me; Adam and Amy got to stay with the campers in the cabins; the Lord moved in a very visible way on the third night of the younger camp.

Over half of the ninety-five campers made some type of commitment at the campfire talk! The next night the genuineness of their decisions was borne out in the testimony time where again, over half of the young campers gave testimony of how the Lord is working in their lives.

OKLAHOMA DEATH ROW

After Bible Memory Camp, Lydia and the children went to a friend's house in Pryor, and I went to prison. The Gospel Echoes were at the maximum-security prison in McAlester, OK (they call it the Big Mac), so I joined the volunteers of the Zion Mennonite Church of Pryor, and went visiting cell-to-cell on death row with them. Some of the most dynamic Christians in God's kingdom are found on death row, but some of the most depraved men I have ever met are there also. One man recognized Glendon Bender as we walked by and asked questions about his family. He knew the children's names and their needs. How? He had been praying for them every day since Glendon was there last year. I gave this old redeemed sinner my card and asked him to pray for me.

I know that many of you pray for this ministry and me regularly, and now I know that one more prayer warrior is lifting us to the throne daily.

As we went past one cell we could hear the man inside screaming and cursing. His face was pressed up against the little bulletproof window, and we could see him from his forehead to his bearded chin. I looked at him as he screamed and lurched at the door, and I felt like I was looking into the face of Satan. Such hatred and seething rage contorted his face and made the veins in his neck bulge. At one time he was a little boy like my precious ten-year-old Adam, but somewhere along the line, he missed God's plan for his life. Instead of praising God with his lips and his life, he is caged up like the animal he has become, and he curses anyone who dares to venture past his door. Can the love of Jesus reach even someone as depraved as this man? I believe it can, and that's the reason that I have the audacity to go into such a hellhole with the gospel of Jesus Christ. His Word does not return void; it saves to the uttermost, and this man was the "uttermostest" that I have ever seen. What confidence we can have in our Lord and Savior Jesus Christ!

SECRETARY

Common Ground Ministries would like to introduce you to our new secretary, Linda Weaver. Linda lives in Mt Hope, just 100 yards from our new office here. She has office experience from her previous job at Hiland Wood Products but is new to prison work. Within the next couple of weeks, she will begin to call on the prison chaplains to schedule our services. Linda and her husband, Joe, are members of the Mt Hope District Amish church. Pray for her as she learns to work with the Ohio Corrections System. We also want to say a special thank you and farewell to Sandi Stoltzfus for staying on with us for over six months until we found a secretary.

June, July - 1995

THOUGHTS ON
THE CLEVELAND INDIANS

The Cleveland Indians won the pennant! And they were in the World Series right up to the last out! What a great season it was for a diehard Indians fan! I'm wondering why an other-wise mature adult like me got so excited and emotional about such a temporal thing as a baseball game. Was it because we have waited so long? Or was it because we took so much teasing and abuse for so many years? Maybe it's because over half of the starters are from Latin America, the culture in which we lived for seven years. Whatever the reason, it was a great season, and I have a few thoughts about this dream team and this year in baseball.

Rather than cool my enthusiasm over such a minor thing as a sporting event, I want to be more excited about eternal things. We are excited about the things that are important to us. Also, I took a lot of good-natured teasing about the Indians over the years. Am I willing to be publicly identified with Jesus Christ, a person that the world considers a loser? If I can take the heat because of a baseball team, surely I can stand up for someone who died for me. And one last thought; I have been an Indians fan through forty years of losing and one year of winning. The year of winning was more fun. I couldn't wait to read the paper each day. Go, Tribe!

In Jesus, we are on the winning side. I can't wait to read His book each day. Praise Jesus!

SIX YEARS OF COMMON GROUND MINISTRIES

At the Common Ground Ministries Fall Banquet we celebrated six years of singing ministry in jails, prisons, overseas, and in many churches and camps here in Ohio. Thank you for six years of faithful support. Without your financial help, we could not reach the thousands of prisoners and other folks that hear our programs and services during the year. Thank you for your faithfulness!

November - 1995

INVITE HIM IN

Last night we were at Chillicothe Correctional. Although it was one day shy of December, we officially started celebrating Christmas. After some opening songs and introductions of our volunteers, I sang some Christmas songs and spoke about the birth of our Savior and how it affects us even to this day, approximately 1995 years later.

I got many comments on this thought: "I don't believe that Christmas is getting commercial." Every year I hear the complaint that Christmas is getting commercial, and although I agree that it is very commercial, I do not accept the premise that it is GETTING commercial. It's always been commercial! It was so commercial the first Christmas that the Lord Jesus Himself could not find a motel, bed & breakfast, hospital, or even a decent place to be born, because of all the tourists. And yet I never read that there was bitterness or complaining on the part of Joseph or Mary, or Jesus Himself after He was old enough to realize that He had had a less than royal birth. The facts were simply stated: "...they laid Him in a manger because there was no room for them in the Inn" (Luke 2:7). They didn't let adverse circumstances spoil the blessed event. And I refuse to let commercialism, Santa Claus, beer commercials, rude shoppers, or anything else ruin this blessed time of the year for my family or me.

I challenged the prisoners not to let their adverse circumstances and separation from their families, etc., keep them from a genuine celebration of the coming of Immanuel, "God with us." Of course it will be hard; of course it would better to be home for Christmas; but you're not. You have a choice: be bitter and angry, or let the miracle of Christmas take place where you are; a prison cell, a place of business, a stressful job, a happy home, a stable turned birthing room... Christ will come in where He is invited. That night in Bethlehem, the only invitation was to a barn. So that's where He went. Invite Him into your life, no matter what the circumstances, and He will come in. A miracle! Merry Christmas!

December - 1995

THIS COULD BE THE YEAR

I know a man who looks out his window every morning and says, "Maybe today..." Maybe today the Lord will come back. Although I don't do that every morning, there is one time I always think of Jesus' return, and that is on the first day of the year. Could this be the year that He will return for His own and take us with Him in what is known as the rapture of the church? What is holding Him back? After studying prophecy and theories of end times (doomsday, according to secular media), I have concluded that the only thing holding back Jesus' return and the beginning of the final judgment can be found in 2 Peter 3:9 – He is "not willing that any should perish..."

In other words, His patience is holding Him back. Which also means that He could come back at any time, even before you finish reading this letter. Are you ready? There is something about the realization that the boss may come back at any moment that makes us want to have our house in order. Jesus may come back this year. It may be today. Living with that expectation keeps us living in hope. If He's coming today, I want to be ready. Since He may come today, I will live today as if He's coming.

1995 WAS A GREAT YEAR

We are beginning our seventh year of singing/prison ministry. Here are a few highlights of 1995:

JANUARY
We Care Prison revival, Atmore, AL

FEBRUARY
Costa Rica Work Mission Trip

APRIL
Pilot's Retreat

JUNE
Bible Memory Camp, Chouteau, OK; Promise Keepers

AUGUST
Little Eden Camp

SEPTEMBER
Men's Bicycle Retreat, NW Ohio

OCTOBER
Revival, Mt. View, VA

NOVEMBER
Couples Retreat, Florida

DECEMBER
Banquets!

We also had forty-five prison services, three camps, various retreats, thirty-plus church services, more than twenty banquets, two recording sessions, a lot of fun, a few defeats, many victories, and hope in the future that makes me very excited about what God is going to do in 1996! After six full years of ministry, our reputation in the Ohio Corrections system is solid, some offers have come in for recording that look exciting, our children are getting to the age where they can minister in our programs, and people's lives are being changed through our ministry. It's going to be a great year!

COLOMBIA, SOUTH AMERICA
Hard work, heat, bugs, boarding with local families, language barrier, frustration, satisfaction, reward... sound like something you've been dreaming of? Pray about coming with us to Cartagena, Columbia, to help build an addition onto a church! Nobody said it would be easy, but I can guarantee that if God wants you to go, it could be the best "vacation" you've ever had!

January - 1996

HORIZON RECORDS

I have signed on to record with the Horizon Music Group, a record company from North Carolina. What this means is that I will record my next project at their studio near Asheville at a slightly higher cost than before, but they will send one of the songs from the recording to more than 1,000 radio stations, and it will be on their record label. The stations may or may not play the song, but at least there is a chance that my music will get airplay and hopefully broaden the ministry of Common Ground Ministries. This is uncharted ground for us, but we are excited at the possibilities. Pray with us that God will use this in a positive way.

NEW RECORDING

Speaking of recording; my newest project, recorded at the Gospel Echoes studio in Goshen, IN, is in Nashville, TN, right now, being duplicated and packaged. It is entitled *ACOUSTIC*, and it is just that—I sing old and new songs, accompanied only by my guitar. It will be released in mid-March.

February - 1996

FROM PROMISE KEEPERS TO PERRYTON, TEXAS

What a contrast! From 42,000 pastors praising and worshipping God in the Georgia Dome to a seventy-member Mennonite Church in the panhandle of Texas! I was privileged to be a part of the historic Atlanta Promise Keepers event in February, possibly the largest gathering of clergy in history, who came to worship and learn how to work together as a church and still keep our particular denominational distinctive. The speakers were a who's who of modern Christian leaders, and the worship was phenomenal. It was a life-changing event.

From Atlanta, I boarded a plane and flew to Amarillo, TX, where I met pastor Darwin Hartman, who drove me through 100 miles of cattle and oil country to his home. I saw more oil wells and cattle than I had seen in my whole life. I went from 42,000 people per acre to 42,000 acres per person! It was a refreshing and needed contrast. The members of that small church welcomed me in like I was a long-lost friend. Maybe it was because we had oil wells on our farm when I was a boy. (I even knew some oil people from nearby Borger, TX.) Maybe it was because I had read stories about the cattle barons; or that I wore cowboy boots; or that they thought I talked like a Texan; or that I was a Cleveland Indians fan and this was Mike Hargrove's hometown.... Whatever it was, we had a great weekend of meetings in the Perryton Mennonite church, and I made new friends in the Lone Star State that will last into eternity.

HUTTONSVILLE CORRECTIONAL AND SARASOTA ENCOUNTER

February 22, 1996. After a Wednesday evening service at Crown Hill Mennonite near Rittman, OH, our family loaded the van and headed for Sarasota, FL, via Huttonsville, WV, where we had one of those rare services where my whole family is allowed to go into the prison. It is the same prison where our son Adam first sang when he was five years old and got such a roaring standing ovation that he looked at me in terror. What had he done wrong to make these prisoners roar and stomp for over a minute? That was the service that it dawned on me that these men have children, too, and they only see them every two weeks at best, and Adam's singing had touched a soft spot in their hearts. God speaks through children, and he did it again on this trip. This time Lydia and all the children sang before I sang and preached. After I gave an invitation because several hands were raised, the chaplain gave another invitation, and at least two of the men gave their hearts to Jesus, and many others came to ask for prayer for their families and their situations.

In Sarasota, I went to four different jails and prisons as an outreach of Encounter '96. In spite of the usual confusion and spiritual enemy activity that goes along with an outsider going into a prison, there were over forty-five recommitments and first-time decisions for Jesus in six services! I could tell that many prayers had gone up for these meetings. And in spite of lower than expected attendance, the Encounter meetings at Ed Smith Stadium were very good, with over 150 young folks making commitments on Friday evening after Steve Wingfield's message on Samson and sexual purity.

On the way home we stopped at Apalachee Correctional Institute in northern Florida (Chaplain Doug Gingerich) and Trenton Correctional Institute in New Holland, SC (Chaplain Sam Mast). Of all the wonderful things we saw and experienced in those two weeks and 3,000 miles, the most beautiful sight on the whole trip was... our front yard! Even buried under two inches of snow, there is no more beautiful sight than home. Can you imagine how wonderful it's going to be to arrive home after journeying here on earth? (Some theologians are saying that there is no snow there.)

March - 1996

DOMINICAN REPUBLIC

"I remember the night I accepted Jesus as my Savior. I was fourteen years old. It was after a youth group talk at The Center in San Jose, Costa Rica. Do you remember that night?"

Joy was looking at me as if I ought to remember.

"I'm afraid I don't remember, Joy."

She was trying to look hurt, but actually, she was surprised.

"You don't remember that night? Well, you were the speaker that night, and you are the one who prayed with me. I realized that I had never received Jesus into my heart even though I grew up in a missionary home..."

This conversation took place last week at Joy's home in Santiago, Dominican Republic, where she and her husband, Bill Mason, and their three children are missionaries at the Santiago Christian School. I was invited to be the speaker at their Spiritual Emphasis Week. What a privilege it was to be the guest of one my former youth group members who is now serving the Lord as a missionary herself! In 1983, after two years of English youth work, Lydia and I were loaned to Young Life International where we worked with Joy's parents for four years in Costa Rica, so she is like a family member as well as a friend to us. It reminded me of one of my axioms for ministry: Eighty percent of success is to keep going. "He that abideth in me, and I in him, the same bringeth forth much fruit." (John 15:5). May we be reminded to keep on keeping on. (Another great axiom: 80% of ministry is just showing up.)

I was in the Dominican Republic from Sunday to Saturday—one school week. I spoke at two chapels a day in the high school while Bill and Joy took care of the three elementary chapels. At the end of the week, twenty-five students raised their hands indicating interest in following Christ, and six students prayed the sinner's prayer out on the schoolyard! Bill and Joy will follow up on these students. It was a great week! Sometimes you just have to show up!

HORIZON MUSIC GROUP

On March 12 I made my first recording with Horizon Records. The project will be entitled *Maximum Security* and is releasing in six to eight weeks. Part of the advantage of being on a label is that one of the songs on the recording will be sent to 1,200 radio stations on a compilation disc—a CD with 8 or 10 different artists. The DJ may or may not play it, but at least it's on his shelf if someone calls requesting it (hint, hint). At this moment, one of my songs, "Golden Love," is on Kevin Spencer's compilation disc, so if you hear Kevin Spencer singing, it is a good chance that my song is somewhere in the studio.

April - 1996

MISSIONS

Of all the people who have ever lived in the history of the world, half of them are alive today!

- J.B. CROUSE
missionary to Korea

If I could choose any time in history to be alive, it would be today.

- DR. DENNIS KINLAW
president of Francis Asbury Society, former president of Asbury College

These two quotes from a missions banquet at the Carlisle Inn in Walnut Creek, OH, on April 27 not only set the tone for the evening but were a reminder of the tremendous privilege and responsibility that our generation has to carry out the great commission in this exciting era in human history. It is possible that more people could come to Jesus Christ in this generation than in all previous generations put together. And if the people of Zion—that's us—don't allow the revival to begin with them, more people could die without Christ in this generation and go to a Christless grave (hell) than at any time in history. What a challenge we have to be all that we can be for Christ! Our call is to go and tell, but only after we stay and listen to—tarry and commune with–the Father.

J.B. and Betty Crouse had just returned from Korea and China the night before I heard them speak. Betty quoted several Chinese Christians: "I would rather die a torturous death than to live one day without Him." ... "Although our lives are in constant danger, it is worth it because of the peace that Jesus gives us."

I long for that kind of relationship with Jesus Christ. Would I rather die than live another day without Him? It is hard in our affluent society to know that kind of devotion, but it is not impossible! May God grant us the desire to know Him and the fellowship of His sufferings. We live in the most exciting era in human history! Let us not miss this moment of opportunity!

PRISON REPORT

Twenty thousand men will be released from prison in Ohio in 1996. Twenty-four thousand will go into Ohio prisons in 1996. The cost of keeping a man in prison for a year would pay his yearly tuition to Ohio State University with room and board, books, laundry, a car, and a chauffeur! Corrections is the biggest item on every state budget in the United States, which means Corrections [sic] is the biggest business in the U.S. Isn't it interesting that we will try anything to fix the problem except that which will work; Jesus Christ? From the year that prayer was taken out of schools and God was taken out of the Supreme Court, the prison population has doubled three times. From nearly 150,000 prisoners in 1960 to 1,230,000 in 1996! Is there a connection between those numbers and the move to get God out of our society? I rest my case. Only proclaiming Christ and putting God back into our society will ever change the need for the tragic system that we call corrections, because only Jesus can truly correct a heart. Napoleon said, "There are two ways to control a man; either the Bible or the bayonet."

May - 1996

ALL THINGS WORK TOGETHER...

One of our goals here at Common Ground Ministries is to minister in as many prisons and other places as we can, provided we have the time, energy, and resources. As hard as we try to control the schedule, now and then the schedule controls us. An example of bad planning occurred the weekend of May 10-12, 1996. My son Adam and I were scheduled to go with a group of men to Promise Keepers in Detroit on Friday, May 10. No problem; I was scheduled to be at Lebanon Correctional just north of Cincinnati the evening before, which is 200 miles away (four hours). One by one all the volunteers canceled. So I would be going alone, I would get home at 2:00 am, and I needed to leave at 5:00 am on Friday... a problem!

I have since learned that a problem is something that can be solved. A fact of life is something you cannot change. This was a solvable problem. My options were:

1. CALL AND CANCEL.
2. GO BY MYSELF.

After deliberation and prayer, I went against the advice of my wise wife and decided that because of the paperwork and hassle to get into a state prison, and because I had committed, I would go even if I would go alone.

It was a beautiful day to travel, and all the way down I sang and prayed and listened to tapes, and wondered what special thing the Lord was going to do in the evening service. I got there right on time and waited ten minutes at the front desk while the man on duty chatted on the phone. He finally spoke.

"Are you in a hurry?"

"I'm here for a chapel service," I said.

"Only one of you showed up? You may as well cancel."

"I drove four hours to get here. I think I'll keep my appointment," I said.

"Can't play all those instruments all by yourself."

I explained, "It's not as much as it looks. Just one guitar and sound equipment."

He got up in slow motion and shuffled around the desk to start the processing, and then he said, "You can't go in. You're wearing blue jeans."

"They're not blue jeans. They're black," I said.

(Ohio prisons have a rule against blue denim jeans because that is what is issued to Ohio inmates to wear, and guards want to be able to distinguish between prisoners and visitors in case of a disturbance.)

"Yeah, but they're denim," he countered,

"But the regulations you sent me say 'no blue jeans.' These are black."

Well, guess who won that discussion. It didn't matter that I had driven four hours by myself. It didn't matter that I was within the guidelines of what they sent and I would never be mistaken for an inmate by my clothes (maybe by my face, but not my clothes). What mattered was that one man could say that I could not get in, so I could not get in.

For the first time in over six years and several hundred prisons, I was refused entrance. (They have since changed the wording to read, "No denim pants.")

I drove four hours home and prayed, first for my attitude, and then for the man at the front desk. Since... "all things work together for good to them that love God" (Romans 8:28), I wondered what good would God bring from this. Then I prayed and sang and listened to tapes all the way home on a beautiful Thursday evening.

And I got home before 2:00 am.

And we had a wonderful time at Detroit Promise Keepers!

June - 1996

THE CHURCHES WILL WORK TOGETHER

It is always good to see churches working together during an Encounter week. Neighboring pastors learn to know and trust each other for the first time since they have been in their churches. Christians of different denominations who work together in every other aspect of community life begin to worship together, sometimes for the first time. What does it take to get Christians to work together?

The truth is, there should always be many more churches involved in Encounter than there are, but distrust, tradition, different doctrinal distinctions, etc., all make it hard for some pastors to work with "that" church. Nothing makes the unchurched person stand up and take notice of a Christian event more than churches working together. "Behold how much better one church is than another..." is not what the Bible says will draw their attention. When we work together, even though we guard and cherish our denominational distinctive, the world will look in and say, "Behold, how they love one another." One of two things will get us to work together: 1. a willingness to reach out and work together in the name of Christ, rather than in the name of our denomination; 2. persecution. It's as simple as that. I vote for #1.

July - 1996

YOU NEVER ASK FOR MONEY

This is an accusation that is not leveled at many Christian ministries. And although I am very happy to be so accused, it is only a half-truth.

The truth is, we do ask for money. We just don't use our newsletter for such purposes. As many of you know, we ask you face-to-face for your support, and your response has been so overwhelming that we have never had to resort to mass appeals for funds via the newsletter. As far as I know, 99 percent of you who support our singing/prison ministry are personal friends of mine who know me, trust me, and believe in what CGM is doing. With God's help, I will never do anything to betray that trust. (Proverbs 22:1). Last fall, when funds got low because of office and secretary expenses that had not been part of our budget before (Leroy Mullet had donated office space for the two previous years), I came to some of you personally, explained the need, and the response was so great that our general fund has been healthy ever since. Because of your generosity, the Common Ground Board can send me to churches, prisons, camps, etc., with the tremendous privilege of not having to ask for a certain fee. That alone gives us a credibility and freedom that larger ministries may not enjoy. What a blessing! Thank you, thank you for your prayer and financial support.

"God's work done in God's way will never lack God's supply."
— HUDSON TAYLOR

CAMPS AND PRISONS

July was a great month! A July 4 gospel singing at the Amish Farm in Berlin, and then off to Onekama, MI, for a week-long family camp at Little Eden Camp where I sang and preached each morning and evening. Even with the responsibilities of being the resource person, it was like a vacation for us as a family. On the way home, Lydia dropped me off at the East Michigan

Wesleyan Camp near Vassar where Steve Wingfield's team was in charge of services. Steve preached every night at the big tabernacle, and each morning Ed Scarce taught two *Share the Life* seminars while I spoke at the two youth meetings. Again, it was hard work as well as a time of refreshing.

I got home in time to sing for a church picnic in Wooster on Sunday afternoon and then a concert with Clearwater Christian Country Band that evening at Mennonite Christian Assembly in Fredericksburg, OH. And wouldn't you know, after singing at a trail ride at Salt Fork State Park on Saturday–I am often mistaken for a cowboy–I ended the month in prison! God is good!

August - 1996

CULTURE SHOCK

"Hey, is that a CD?"

I was setting up the equipment at Grafton Correctional last Sunday when I heard that question. As I put the compact disc soundtrack in the player, Jim came up like a curious child, staring at the compact disc.

"I've heard about these CDs for a long time, but I've never seen one. Is that what they look like? How do they work?"

I took it out of the player and let him look at it, and explained what I knew about it, and he looked it over like it was a rare coin, gave it back to me, and then he went back to his seat with a look of wonder on his face.

CDs have been out for more than fifteen years! This man has been behind bars for so long that he has never seen a compact disc. I wonder what else he has never seen. I remember coming back from Costa Rica after seven years and seeing all the things that were already commonplace here in the States; video games, computers, remote controls, and yes, CDs. I know a little of what Jim was feeling. When I would ask questions about the new things, people would ask, "Where have you been, man?" I would tell them I had been in Costa Rica, and that would usually end up in a pleasant conversation and even an opportunity to witness for Christ. I was made to feel like a returning hero or a person of honor. What's going to happen to Jim when he gets out of Grafton and answers the question, "Where have you been, man?" "I've been in prison, man." Will that end up in a pleasant conversation?

If these men are not solidly grounded in Jesus Christ, their chances for survival in the free world are slim. They will have as much culture shock coming back to their homes and communities as we did when we first went to San Jose, Costa Rica, a foreign culture to us.

For fifteen years Jim has been in an environment where every move is governed by a whistle or a bell or someone telling him what to do. Many times, because of compassionate laws, inmates are not required to work. After fifteen years of laying in your bunk or lifting weights whenever you feel like it, eight hours of solid work seems like a long time. And the pay for an entry-level job in the free world after working forty hours in a week doesn't go very far. He used to make that much in one hour when he was doing illegal activities on the street! The system doesn't prepare men for life in the real world. Sometimes I think it almost guarantees failure, a return to prison, and another ruined life at $20,000 a year at our expense.

Jesus Christ will not only change a man's life and help prepare him for a life of freedom, but the gospel makes good economic sense. To control a man's actions with the word of God is a lot cheaper, saner, and honorable than controlling him at one of our state institutions. Napoleon said there are two ways to control a man: The Bible or the bayonet. Jim and 20,000 men like him are going to be released from Ohio prisons in 1996. Which kind of man would you want in your community; one who is struggling to follow Christ and needs your help (i.e., discipleship), or one who needs outside forces (i.e., police, prison) to keep him under control?

The next time you buy a CD, pray for men like Jim. Pray for the institutions. Pray for ministries like ours, that we might present Christ in such a way that men like Jim can become functional, useful, Godly citizens. They're coming soon to a community near you!

September - 1996

PEACE IN PRISON

I am writing this from Columbia, PA, where Encounter '96 and Steve Wingfield have brought me for ten days. On the way from Ohio, I stopped at a prison to visit a man who is in for murder. He told me that he had lost all hope, especially when he thought of the terrible thing he had done. He then found Jesus Christ in prison (actually, Jesus found him. Jesus wasn't lost; this man was), but he still struggled with forgiveness. How could God forgive such an evil deed? He was having the same struggles that slave trader John Newton had. The only way that God could forgive such evil was through His "Amazing Grace," as in the song written by John Newton. This prisoner told me, "I have finally found peace. I never had such peace and freedom before. I am finally free!"

I hear this story over and over, and it never gets old and never fails to amaze and encourage me. Why wait to go to prison to find His peace? My prayer is that you will encourage someone to seek Him while He may be found and thus experience the peace that passes understanding.

October - 1996

DEATH ROW

What a privilege to see my family on death row! Sound strange? It's amazing how one of the worst, most hopeless places on earth can be a blessing when you're in the right relationship with Jesus Christ.

We went to the Delaware Correctional Center at the invitation of Nelson Coblentz, who was holding a three-day prison revival. While he was in the prison chapel on Tuesday night, my family and I, alnog with some volunteers, went to the section of the prison called "pre-trial" and held simultaneous services. Then, on Wednesday, we had a service at the Greenwood Mennonite Church while Gospel Express was to be at pre-trial. We had a great time at the Greenwood church service, but the scheduled service at the prison was canceled due to an unscheduled   escape attempt! A convicted murderer had been let out of maximum security into the general population and promptly tried to escape. Nelson and the volunteers returned from supper to find helicopters, police cars, and news reporters surrounding the prison. They were politely informed that there would be no service that night.

On Thursday our family, the Coblentz family, and the volunteers went to the maximum security section ("the hole," solitary confinement, death row), and went from cell to cell singing, sharing, and handing out literature. It was the first time that Lydia and my children had ever been in such a place. We sang loud enough to penetrate the thick steel doors of the prison, and Adam, Amy, Katie, and little Megan Coblentz sang so loud and sweet that it penetrated the thick doors of many hard hearts behind the tattooed chests of rough-looking men. When the children sang, a smile and a tear crossed the faces of most of the men. One hard-looking man was trying to maintain his mean look, but I saw his foot tapping under the door, and when I pointed to his foot he couldn't suppress a smile. What a privilege to have my family as ministers: "From the lips of children and infants you, Lord, have called forth your praise"; Jesus quoting Psalm 8:2 (Matthew 21:16 NIV). There were many commitments to Jesus Christ. One man said, "Thanks for bringing your children." (Note: In the Ohio prison system, you must be eighteen to enter, so the children don't go in here.)

MOTORHOME

And speaking of having my family as part of the ministry... we are now the excited, happy owners of a 29-foot 1996 Jayco motorhome! After much prayer and discussion with the board, it was decided that in order to keep my family as involved as possible, a bus or motorhome would be a wise investment. I met with Bertha Bontrager Rhodes, owner of Jayco, Inc. in Middlebury, IN, and she gave us a fantastic offer on a 1996 prototype RV. I then came to many of you to express the need, and in less than two weeks you had given and pledged enough money to be able to take Bertha up on her generous offer! I have the unusual privilege to use this letter to give praise rather than to ask you to give. Thank you for that privilege. It gives our ministry and the Lord credibility, it encourages us, AND we have a motorhome! Going to the Delaware prison was our first trip. Thank you!

November - 1996

ARE THERE CATS IN PARADISE?

A busy November saw us in Delaware, Florida, Oklahoma, and Pennsylvania for a prison, a board meeting, a couple's retreat, and a missions conference. As I was unloading the equipment at Paradise Mennonite Church in Pennsylvania, I reached into the luggage bay of our motorhome and out jumped our neighbor's cat! Charlie must have crawled in the night before while we were loading up at home, which means he was in that dark compartment for about twenty hours. It took me almost thirty minutes to catch him with the help of some deer bologna that we had with us, but he was in good shape! He was put into darkness in Holmes County and woke up in Paradise!

CHRISTMAS IS FOR CHILDREN

Have you ever heard the phrase: "Christmas is for children"? If your children are like ours, it is not hard to understand where that saying originated. I love to see the excitement in my children's eyes and hear it in their voices during this season. We have some family traditions that have developed at this time of the year because of our children: a tree in the house; driving around to look at lights; taking cookies to neighbors... But the whole truth is that as much as I love to observe our kids during this season, Christmas is not just for children. It's for everyone.

As I think of the U.S. prison population, I think that if more men had realized that Christmas is for mature adults, several million children would have their daddy's at home on December 25. They could celebrate the birth of Jesus with them and witness the sparkle in their eyes, instead of phone calls, visits, letters, or... silence. (Some men cut off contact with children out of shame, guilt, or how hurtful it is to see them through prison bars.)

Is Christmas just for children? Well, if you mean "childlike"— as opposed to "childish"—then I will agree that Christmas is for children. Jesus said, "Verily I say unto you, except ye be converted, and become as little children, ye shall not enter into the kingdom of heaven" (Matthew 18:3). We must receive Jesus like a little child. So, yes, Christmas is for children!

God has poured out His blessings on us in this last year. May you receive the Christ-child in childlike faith.

December - 1996

1997

HAPPY NEW YEAR!

"Though outwardly we are wasting away, yet inwardly we are being renewed day by day" (2 Corinthians 4:16 NIV).

I think of this verse every New Year's Eve. Another year! My parents used to tell me that life goes fast. I always thought the old fogeys didn't know what they were talking about but now that I'm on the western side of forty, time seems to go faster and my body goes slower even though I am in excellent health—I rode my bicycle twenty miles today. As usual, Mom and Dad were right. If this physical life were all I had to look forward to, I would probably join the health craze and try to stay young as long as I could. Even though I try to take care of this vessel of clay, I realize that my parents were right and the scriptures are true—I am wasting away—but only outwardly!

Inwardly—in my spirit—I am being renewed day by day! What a comfort and what a reason to not despair! This physical life is not all there is! In this last year, more than twenty people that I knew personally died. They wasted away. Inwardly, many of them are still being renewed day by day (in Heaven). Are you?

You don't have to be on the western slope to realize that this physical life won't last forever. Some of those funerals were for young people. I challenge you this year to make sure that your reservations are in for your eternal home in Heaven. Invite Jesus into your heart right now if you don't know Him personally. If you do know Him, recommit yourself to renewing your spirit day by day. Make 1997 your year of renewal! "Give'em Heaven in '97!"

January - 1997

WE CARE PRISON REVIVAL

In January we headed for Montgomery, AL, for a four-day prison revival with We Care Ministries. I was in six different prisons and had eight services in those four days. One of the most memorable moments was after Lydia and the children sang at the Birmingham Women's Work Release Facility.

A man came up and said, "I watched your program with mixed emotions. I was encouraged to see your family singing together, but at the same time, I was saddened because when I was your age, I wasn't much of a father. I was deep in sin and seldom at home and as a result, I lost my two oldest children. I became a Christian in time to have a good relationship with my youngest."

And then he said, "Son, keep doing what you're doing. If more fathers would be priests in their home like you are, these prisons would be empty."

It is always a joy to hear encouraging words, and I too had mixed emotions for this man. I rejoiced that he was walking with the Lord and that our family was an inspiration to him, but I grieved that his oldest children wanted nothing to do with him. I reminded him of what God said through the prophet Joel, *I will restore to you the years that the locust hath eaten...* This man was one of the We Care volunteers and is an active prison minister in his home state. God is restoring to him the years that he so tragically squandered, and I believe God will give back to his children the inborn love for their daddy that they gave to someone else in his absence. Pray for this man.

And pray for We Care president Phil Weber and the great work done by this ministry in Atmore, AL. Over 250 volunteers from all over the U.S. and Canada came and for four days invaded Satan's turf in those prisons. Many prisoners became followers of Jesus Christ, and many volunteers will never be the same; "you know that your labor in the Lord is not in vain" (1 Corinthians 15:58 NIV). I like to say it this way: "Ninety percent of prison ministry is simply SHOWING UP."

INTERNATIONAL POULTRY CONVENTION

You may be asking the same question that a Holmes County businessman asked me when he saw me at the largest poultry convention in the U.S. in Atlanta, GA.; "What in the world are you doing here?" I think that's a fair question since the last time I had anything to do with the poultry industry was at age eleven when I gathered eggs from our chicken coop where we had about twenty-eight chickens (although I am directly involved with the industry every time I eat at Der Dutchman Restaurant). This convention had 26,000 attendees and over 2,000 company displays!

I was there at the invitation of Gerald Strite, President of Shenandoah Manufacturing from Harrisonburg, VA. We got to know each other when he was on the Steve Wingfield Ministries Board. I sang at his company's award breakfast there on Thursday morning, which turned out to be a wonderful time of fun and inspiration.

I believe that the 120 people who attended that business awards breakfast were refreshed by God's Spirit as He allowed me to sing fun, secular songs along with stories and testimony of God's working in my life and in the lives of prisoners. It was obvious that these businessmen have come to expect high morals and a spiritual uplift when they deal with Shenandoah, as many of them stopped at Gerald's booth throughout the morning to express appreciation for the inspiration. May more businesses have such a reputation. This type of meeting fits exactly the Common Ground Ministries philosophy; "Sharing Christ through song."

February - 1997

COLOMBIA

Last month I wrote that if all went well, I would be in Colombia, South America, as you read this letter. All went well, and as you were reading last month's letter, I was in Cartagena, Colombia, with thirteen other hard-working, adventurous short-term missionaries, building classrooms for a church/school. We had a great time as we stayed in Colombian homes, ate their food, worked all day, and attended their church services every night. (Yes, they had church almost every night!)

I preached six times and interpreted one night as Roy Miller preached. I spoke enough Spanish to give me a headache! We accomplished quite a bit on the building that will be used for Sunday School rooms on Sunday and a Christian School during the week. We were also able to give over $2,000.00 to buy materials for the construction. Thank you for praying for us.

AMELIA BYLER, 83

Two days before Lydia and our girls were to leave for Costa Rica to meet Adam and me coming from Colombia, I called home to find that Mom Byler (Lydia's mother) was very sick and we'd better rethink our plans. We canceled the tickets, would get them reissued when Mom rallied, and then on Friday afternoon, February 7, Amelia Byler entered into the presence of the Lord. I got the word very soon after that and was able to change Adam's and my tickets and come home one day early, just in time to be with the family for the second day of calling hours and the funeral. Because Mom got very sick, all the children but one were able to come and say goodbye and have quality time with her in her last hours, even through her suffering. The funeral was a victory celebration because of a life lived for Christ, although she will be greatly missed by children and grandchildren as well as many friends; she left a legacy of love and faithfulness.

Note: With a not too small fine and re-issue fee, our family will be able to use the Costa Rica tickets in March. Also, two weeks to the day of Amelia's death, her brother Ed Gingerich died in Iowa.

March - 1997

WHY DO WE KEEP DOING WHAT WE ARE DOING?

Chuck Colson was in Cleveland, OH, last month and spoke about the prison system and our society and what is happening as we get farther and farther away from God. As he closed his brilliant talk, he let us know that tomorrow he would be in Baltimore, MD, the next day in Washington, D.C., the next day in Minneapolis, MN, the next day... etc. Then he asked the rhetorical question; "Why do I do this?" Colson is over sixty years of age and would be financially able to retire and relax. He could make more money from his books than most of us will make in our lifetime. So, it was a fair question. Why would someone of Colson's stature and stage in life go in to what our society considers the cesspools of society; our prisons?

People have asked me the same question. Sometimes I'm asked out of curiosity, sometimes out of suspicion—there must be money in prison ministry—and sometimes out of a sincere desire to know how to discern God's perfect will for one's life. I think the reasons that Colson gave are worth repeating.

Here is why he proclaims Christ in prisons and anywhere he is invited to speak:

Out of gratitude. God saved Colson just before he went to prison in the early '70s and he has never forgotten that.

Compassion. Nor has he forgotten the men who were with him in prison.

A sense of God's call. It's not just the need. If we only responded to the need, we would all be in Calcutta or Haiti or Africa, because that's where the need is the greatest. The need is not the call. But when God calls us to service, we will never be satisfied doing anything else. We may be happy and comfortable in life, but something will be missing until we answer the call.

A Jewish tradition tells of a man who used to stand outside Sodom and Gomorrah yelling and proclaiming that they should repent. Day after day he would stand there, yelling and screaming, "Repent! Repent! Turn to God! Change your ways!"

One day a young man came by and said to the man, "What good do you think you're doing? They're never going to repent, and you know it. Why do you continue to scream? Why don't you just quit?"

The man answered, "Maybe you're right. They may never change. But I keep on screaming so that they don't change me."

Now maybe that's not the best reason to keep doing what we're doing, but on those days when it seems like nothing is going right and plans don't come together—like our Bill Glass Weekend of Champions in Fresno, CA, being cancelled one hour before I was to leave for the airport—it helps to fall back on this old Jewish story.

They may not change because of our ministry, but we keep proclaiming so they don't change us!

April - 1997

SPANISH PRISON SERVICE

For the first time since I'm home from Costa Rica, I participated in a Spanish worship service. And it was in prison! Noble County Correctional is a new facility and is in such a rural area where there are no Latinos that there had been no Spanish services for the Latin population there. I mentioned to the chaplain that I used to live in Central America and would be glad to lead a Spanish service, and he took me up on it.

Yesterday (June 1) former Central American volunteers Owen Troyer, Randy Keim, and David Miller went with me to Noble prison. After the regular Sunday morning worship and dinner at a local restaurant, we came back into the prison for the first Spanish service ever to be held at Noble Correctional, to begin at 1:00 pm. Nobody was sure what to expect. At 1:00 pm the chapel was empty. At 1:01 pm, men started filing in with shouts of *"Dios te bendiga!"* and *"Adorado sea el Senor!"* About forty men whose first language is Spanish (and three or four curious English-speaking men) came for a time of singing, testimony, and preaching in their native tongue.

Five different nations were represented in the congregation. Even with our accented Spanish, I saw tears in eyes of some of the men as they heard the gospel in their own language for the first time since they had been incarcerated; some for the first time ever. Although their participation was not as lively as a typical Costa Rican service, the response to the invitation was overwhelming.

One of the non-Latin prisoners told us after the service that although he could not understand anything, he came because he saw how excited the Latinos were all week anticipating the service, and he wanted to come and be a part of what was going to happen. He said he felt the Spirit of God in the service. *Gloria a Dios!*

INTERNATIONAL SERVICE

A prison congregation is not a typical church. In addition to being full of convicted criminals as well as redeemed sinners, it also has an international flavor that is seldom seen in the typical U.S. church. Last week at Mercer Correctional in Pennsylvania, our volunteers were heard speaking Pennsylvania Dutch to one inmate; there were Spanish speakers in the crowd; there were blacks and whites worshipping together, and on the front bench was a man who wept as I sang "Jerusalem." He shouted during the songs, "Via Dolorosa" and "The Eastern Gate." I found out that he was a Christian Arab from Jerusalem, Israel, who spoke Hebrew and Arabic. I don't know what kind of trouble he got himself into over here, but it's interesting that God prompted me to tell of my pilgrimage to the Holy Land and sing the songs of Zion on the very night that a native of that land would be seeking for hope and forgiveness. He said that he is sure that the God of Israel sent me to Mercer Correctional.

June - 1997

E PLURIBUS UNUM

You have heard that money talks, but unless you understand Latin, you may not hear every one of our U.S. coins saying, *E Pluribus Unum* (Out of many, One). Ever notice the Latin phrase above the Lincoln Memorial on a penny? This was the philosophy and ideal of our forefathers; to bring people together from many different backgrounds under one idealistic government where the goal would be liberty and justice for all. That was quite a radical idea!

Or was it? *Radical,* according to Webster, means "extreme." But it also means *1. arising from or going to a root source: BASIC.*

Isn't it interesting that going back to the original or root source is considered radical? What was the American patriot's root source? Are you ready for a radical answer? It was the Bible! Our American forefathers got their ideas from the source of Life, the Word of God; this particular thought, *e Pluribus Unum,* is so similar to the call of Abraham in Genesis 12, that I don't think it is coincidence. God called Abraham and told him, "I will make you into a great nation..." and all peoples on earth will be blessed through you (Genesis 12:2 NIV). *E Pluribus Unum!* Although the Jews became God's people throughout the Old Testament, and still are, God's desire was for the whole world. Jesus clarified this in His conversation with Nicodemus; "For God so loved the world... that whosoever believes in Him shall not perish... (John 3:16). In John 17, Jesus prayed for the ones who would believe in Him "that they may be one as we are one."

I was thinking of this not only because of the July 4 holiday, but because, in June, we had visitors: my college roommate from Alabama, and friends from Costa Rica and Columbia. A few Amish cousins from Kansas stopped in, as did tourists we met when they came to our church on a Sunday night several years ago. In the prisons, we see men from all walks of life, every race, economic level, and social class. In our travels, we meet all kinds of people. And although I don't usually go around thinking, "Boy, e Pluribus Unum," I do think quite often, "Christ died for that person, too."

No matter what nationality, race, economic level, or background, etc., we all have a common malady: sin. And we all have a solution: Christ. Knowing that God's word is true not only for a middle-class white American but also for a tribal chief in Africa and a gang leader in Chicago, I have the confidence to go anywhere in the world, even prisons, and proclaim God's love. The tribal chief, the gang leader, the middle-class white man... all have the same God-given needs: recognition, acceptance, meaning in life, and love. These can only be found in Christ.

This July 4, as we celebrate the freedom and liberty that was won at the Revolutionary War at great cost, and the freedom that gave my German ancestors the liberty to come here and be American citizens, may we remember that Christ won a greater, costlier battle that gives everyone, no matter who you are, the freedom to become citizens of heaven. Make your "Declaration of Dependence" (on Christ) today! *E Pluribus Unum.*

July - 1997

SOMERSET PRISON

"Este era nuestro primer culto en espanol aqui en esta carcel!
Que Bueno! Ojala que regreses!" ("This was our first Spanish
service in this prison. How good it was! Come back!")

— SOLOMON
inmate at Somerset prison.

At the Somerset prison service—part of the Mifflin County
Encounter '97 prison outreach—Chaplain Phil Maust lament-
ed that he had not planned a Spanish service. He said he had
forgotten that I had lived in Latin America, and there has been
no Spanish service here for a long time. I said, "I'm free tomorrow and Wednesday." Even though it is very unusual in
the prison system to plan anything without two weeks notice,
I saw Phil's eyes saying, "Maybe we could do it."

At the risk of being laughed at or even reprimanded by the
monstrous bureaucracy in prison, Phil put in a request for us
to come back in two days for a Spanish service. Because it
was a Spanish service, and because the Catholic chaplain also
went to bat for us, we were granted permission. Since Chaplain Phil didn't work on Tuesday, the Catholic chaplain was
the one who gladly spread the word among the Spanish-speaking inmates. On Wednesday evening we returned and had a
small congregation of ten men. Even with my accented Spanish, they felt like someone from home was with them. We
sang, talked informally, and I spoke about Jesus from a story
in Mark. Five countries were represented by those ten men.
Three of them rededicated their lives to Christ.

Afterward, several of the men were gathered around and one
of them asked, "What kind of Catholic are you? You're different." Because the Catholic chaplain had been the one who

announced the service, they all assumed they were coming to mass. The word 'catholic' means 'universal,' so I told them, "I'm a Biblical Catholic." I belong to the church universal, so I figured I had told them the truth.

LAZY BUSY DAYS OF SUMMER

July started out with a bang (July 4) and ended up with a fifteen-hour drive from Onekama, MI, to New Holland, PA, to sing at the wedding reception of a good friend. In between those two dates I was involved in two evangelistic crusades (Nelson Coblentz in Holmes County, OH, and Steve Wingfield in Mifflin County, PA), six prison services (one of them in Spanish), a Promise Keepers Wake Up Call in Lancaster, PA, an Indians baseball game, a high school reunion, a company picnic, and a week-long family camp in Michigan, where I was camp speaker twice a day. What a blessed, busy July! Many people came to Jesus in the crusades and in the prison services. It makes all the travel and work involved worth it! We are tired and happy.

As we traveled the 1,670 miles in our motorhome, I couldn't help but think of those of you who so generously helped us with the purchase price of this vehicle. It makes travel with the family so much easier and allows us to be much more effective in our ministry. May God bless you for your generosity.

August - 1997

CYCLE OF MINISTRY

We are in our motorhome on the way home from a church retreat in Blountstown, which is in the Northern Panhandle of

Florida. We have been enjoying 90-degree heat at a camp with one hundred or so members of Bethel Mennonite Church. The series of events, which has brought us to this little town four times in the last several years, is worth sharing.

In July 1991 my Sunday School teacher friend Doug Gingerich went with me to prison, partly because he noticed the changed life of our friend Ken Wengerd who recommitted his life to Christ at the Holmes County Encounter '91. Later, at a prison seminar at the Indiana State Prison, Doug recommitted his life to Christ when the speaker, Glendon Bender, gave the invitation on Sunday morning. Within two years, he sold his business, sold his house, gave up his chair at the local coffee shop, and moved his family to Florida where he worked as a volunteer chaplain at Apalachee Correctional under the Gospel Express Supply Chaplain program.

While working as a volunteer and raising his own support, he attended classes at a nearby college and earned a theology degree, which made him eligible to apply for the position of a state chaplain (paid by the state). So after working as a chaplain for three-and-a-half years for no pay, he has now been a paid staff chaplain for the last six months and, starting Friday, September 5, 1997, he will be installed as head chaplain over the two correctional institutions at Appalachee! He attends the Bethel Mennonite Church where he is on the pastoral team, and in that capacity, he invited us down this weekend to speak and sing at their annual retreat. We had a great time.

From construction company owner who taught Sunday School to head chaplain over two prisons and associate pastor at Bethel Mennonite! God works in mysterious ways, but notice in the account above how many different ministries contributed to Doug's pilgrimage: Berlin Mennonite Church; Common Ground Ministries; Steve Wingfield Encounter Ministries; Gospel Echoes Prison Ministries; and the Gospel Express Evangelistic Team, along with Doug's parents, as well as Ken Wengerd and other friends.

LESSON: We are in this together. It's amazing what God can do through us if we're not concerned with who gets the credit. And what a pleasure and privilege it is to work in harness with other ministries rather than in competition with them. We serve the same Lord.

"If you sow and do not reap, someone will reap after you. Be faithful.

If you reap having not sown, someone sowed before you. Be humble."

—STEVE WINGFIELD
September - 1997

A VISIT FROM HOME

At the Noble County Correctional unit on September 6, we again held two services; one in English and one in Spanish. I hadn't ventured to hold a Spanish service in the ten years that I've been home from Costa Rica until June of this year, when the chaplain at Noble Correctional wondered if I knew of anyone who could come in and minister to the Latin prisoners. There had been no Spanish church service there since the prison opened a year ago because they are so far from a big city. I mentioned that I used to speak Spanish, but it is rusty and accented. He said, "Please come! That will be better than nothing, and in the land of the blind, a one-eyed man is king!" So this "one-eyed" man spoke and stuttered about the King of Kings three months ago at that prison and since that time, I have preached and sung in Spanish four different times! Last Sunday (September 21) I even spoke at a Spanish church in Kennett Square, PA, as part of the Chester County Encounter '97.

While I was tearing down the equipment after the Noble Prison service, one of the inmates who had been there in the June service, said, "Seeing you here again is like a visit from home!" Amazingly, someone had said that same thing in the morning English service! No one in prison had ever said that to me in eight years of prison ministry, because a chapel service and a personal visit are vastly different to a prisoner, and now two different men from two different cultures and countries and languages said it in the same day! I think God was trying to tell me something.

CONCLUSIONS:

Inmates crave visits. "I was in prison, and you visited me." (Matthew 25:36)

Ninety percent of success in ministry is showing up. "Better a neighbor nearby than a relative far away." (Proverbs 27:10)

We are beginning to make inroads of trust in the inmates' lives by consistently showing up. "Those who have been given a trust must prove faithful." (1 Corinthians 4:2)

Your faithful support and prayer makes our showing up possible (and a joy). "How are they to preach unless they are sent?" (Romans 10:15)

Jesus will use your talents (even Spanish) if you give them to Him. "Here is a boy with five small barley loaves and two small fish, but how far will they go among so many?" (John 6:9 NIV).

October - 1997

OCTOBER REPORT

We went to Washington D.C. on October 4 to be a part of the Promise Keepers "Stand in the Gap" Rally on the Mall near the Capitol Building. What a sight! Congress has passed a law forbidding the Park Service from estimating the size of a crowd because of a threatened lawsuit after the Million Man March, and I am no expert, but there were a bunch of men there! Unofficial estimates range anywhere from one million to two-and-a-half million. One Park Service worker said he was not allowed to estimate size, but it was the biggest crowd he had seen in his twenty-four years in Washington. What an experience to be in a worship service with a crowd so big that 30,000 of them could not even get on the mall! And getting there on a bus full of friends and men from other churches was half the fun.

From Washington we went to Grand Rapids, MI, for a mission's conference and then to Charm, Ohio, for Charm Days! To complete this gamut of different events, our family sang at the Transport for Christ Annual Banquet near Buffalo, NY, and then three banquets in one week here at home (including our own Annual Appreciation Banquet in Walnut Creek, which turned out to be a great night!). We ended the month with a prison, a hayride, and a benefit concert near Berlin.

It is because of friends like you that we are able to report the very typical month's activities above. Your steady, faithful financial and prayer support have enabled us to be able to go to churches and prisons without having to ask for a fee. This not only gives us opportunity to minister in big places as well as small, but in a day of suspicion toward certain ministries, it gives us credibility. Thank you.

November - 1997

UNTO US A SAVIOR IS BORN

Dear Friends,

Season's Greetings from our family to yours! As we see 1997 pass into history and anticipate 1998 and what opportunities God will open for us, I realize more and more that history is inseparable from "His story." The very numbers that we call dates which we had to memorize in history class are reminders of how long it has been since Jesus walked the face of our planet...

1066...1492...1776...1803...1863...1945...1974...

Each date commemorates an event that occurred and tells how many years it's been since Jesus was here physically. One day, about 1,997 years ago, an angel appeared to a young girl in Israel telling her gospel (good news), and the Holy Spirit "overshadowed" her so that she would be the bearer of Emmanuel, "God with us." All of history hinges on that event and all of His story will eventually come to pass. What a privilege it is to be called to be a bearer of that good news (gospel) to a world that desperately needs the hope that only the Christ child can bring.

I, along with Lydia and the children, thank each one of you for your prayers, financial support, physical presence, and friendship as Common Ground Ministries begins its eighth year on January 1, 1998. I know that God could have done it some other way, but He chose to call me to go and He asked you to support, and because of your obedience and willingness to be involved, I can honestly say that these last seven years, even with the usual knocks and rough spots, have been a blast! They have been some of the best years of my life. Thank you!

In this Christmas season, may we be reminded that *He rules the world with truth and grace, and He makes the nations prove the glories of His righteousness and wonders of His love... and wonders of His love... and wonders, wonders of His love.*

Joy to the world, the Lord is come!

Let earth receive her King!

Let every heart prepare Him room!

And what would be the result if *every heart prepared Him room?*

Heaven and nature (would) sing!

With God's help and yours, we will continue to proclaim Christ until Heaven and nature sing!

MERRY CHRISTMAS
AND A HAPPY NEW YEAR!

December - 1997

TIME FLIES

On your grandfather clock, you may have noticed the Latin inscription, *Tempus fugit* (time flies). The "tempus" really "fugit-ed" this past year and I have great memories of prisons services, mission trips, camps, banquets, family time, excitement... a great year!!

Part of the reason for my excitement and energy is that I am learning more and more to wait on the Lord, and He promises that if we will wait on Him "we will mount up (fly) with wings like eagles. We will run and not be weary, we will walk and not faint." We ran and flew (and sometimes walked) right through 1997 and we didn't get weary.

Another reason for the renewed energy is that I believe I am doing what God wants me to do, and when you are doing the very thing that God created you for, there is peace, energy, purpose, satisfaction... and enthusiasm. (Enthusiasm = "in God")

A third reason for excitement about the coming year is Vision. Without a vision, the people perish. God has given me a vision for 1998. Let me share it with you.

For the past two years or so, God has blessed Common Ground Ministries in many ways:

- We are gaining favor with chaplains and officers in the Ohio prison system

- We have seen many changed lives among the inmate population; (one guard told me that even when it doesn't look like anything happened in chapel, there is a difference in the attitude and mood of the prison after we've been there.

- We have taken mission teams to Latin America

- Finances have been steady

- Opportunities for camps, weekend meetings, banquets, and evangelistic meetings have multiplied

God has blessed our ministry and we see fruit and signs of God's approval. For over a year now I have actually been comfortable. Now, being comfortable is the American dream, and I am an American, and yes, it has been great, but the Bible warns, "Woe to those who are at ease in Zion" (Amos 6:1 ESV). There is so much to do and we are still just scratching the surface of what could be done in prisons, in missions, and even here in our own community.

Our vision? Get out of the comfort zone and out on the edge. We have several aspects to our 1998 vision, but here is the focus: After much prayer and counsel, our board has approved taking the first steps to look into the possibility of hiring another full-time worker to work with Common Ground Ministries. We believe that another worker would more than double our effectiveness. There is a need for more seminars in prisons, more help with the Bible study courses, more speaking opportunities... the possibilities are many.

This would mean more than doubling our budget and many other adjustments, so we covet your prayers and counsel. It will definitely take us out of the comfort zone and put us out on the cutting edge, but if God is in it, resources will not be an obstacle. We have a man in mind for this position and we will keep you informed as we try to discern what our next move is. Pray for us.

"If you're not living on the edge, you're taking up too much space!"

January - 1998

WE CARE PRISON REVIVAL, ATMORE, ALABAMA

Blountstown, Florida, January 9: After a great concert with the Inspirations at Bahia Vista Mennonite Church in Sarasota, we headed north to Alabama where I led a seminar at the Sunday orientation for 200 We Care volunteers who came from all over the U.S. to go into 15 different prisons in the Montgomery/

Birmingham/Northern Florida area. That same evening we headed the 3-1/2 hours back south to Blountstown where we would spend three days in three different Florida prisons.

Hometown boy Doug Gingerich was the head chaplain at two of the prisons where we had services. What a joy to be working in prison with a chaplain who used to be my Sunday School teacher, who used to be in our Bible Study, who is a close friend, and who rededicated his life to Christ as a volunteer in a prison service!

I had chapel services each night in three different prisons. During the day we wandered through the prison yard, talking to whoever would stop to talk with us (and even some who wouldn't). One man told me that his wife and son visited him and after she left the prison, they drove to a nearby 76 truck stop to get gas. When his wife got back in the car after paying the gas, her son was missing. She searched frantically and then called the police. After a short search, they found the 8-year-old boy on the Interstate ramp, hitchhiking back to the prison "to see daddy." This man is a convicted felon. But to an 8-year-old boy, he is daddy. When a man goes to prison, a family goes to prison.

Each night we saw men come forward to make commitments and recommitments to Christ. I was only one of ten different singing groups that week. There were also many preachers and speakers there to proclaim the love and forgiveness of Jesus. Would you like to be involved? Let me know. It will change your life and it may change the lives of some desperate, lonely men.

MISSION TRIPS

Colonia Blanca, Costa Rica, February 1998. We are teaming up with Harold and Debbie Troyer, who have led five teams since 1993, to take a work team down to Costa Rica.

Nineteen of us from Wayne and Holmes Counties are going down to do construction, evangelism, visiting, and have an eye-opening trip to gain vision into what God is doing in His world.

This is the busiest three months of our nine-year-old ministry. Florida, Alabama, back to Florida, Mexico, Pennsylvania, California, Costa Rica, Texas, Florida, Israel, and then back to Florida again! It's hard work. I'm tired and I love it!

"Pray also for me, that whenever I speak, words may be given me so that I will fearlessly make known the mystery of the gospel." (Ephesians 6:19 NIV)

February - 1998

A WORD

by Ken Wengerd

"Do you have a word for me?" Hobard asked me that question two weeks ago at the J.O. Davis Correctional facility near Atmore, Alabama. He did not want to know about salvation. He was already saved. He was looking for encouragement to walk in victory inside the walls of prison. This small request evoked a surge of emotions as I reflected on a "word" we received almost seven years ago.

The year was 1991. It was a hot June evening. We were seated twelve rows back from the stage inside a white and yellow striped tent near Berlin, Ohio. Steve Wingfield had just spoken a message about turning your family's life over to God. That night Brenda and I turned everything over to Jesus Christ. Our lives have not been the same since.

The very next night I went with John Schmid to the Pickaway Correctional Facility near Orient, Ohio. My first time in prison was scary. I hid behind speakers, sat in the back row and did not make eye contact with anyone. What a difference a little time and a lot of encouragement has made!

Since that night many people have had a word for us. The two years we spent at Rosedale Bible Institute has also prepared us for the ministry. It was great to be constantly growing and learning in our walk with Christ. Thank you for your continued support and words of encouragement.

So what did I tell Hobart? For physical training is of some value, but godliness has value for all things, holding promise for both the present life and the life to come (I Timothy 4:8). Godliness is the way to go. Our goal must be constantly striving towards living a Godly life no matter where we are.

WE'VE GOT A PROBLEM

Dr. Cooke of the Florida Correctional Central Office gave us some sad statistics during the Gospel Express prison blitz in

North Florida last week. There are over 64,000 prisoners in Florida in sixty-two major prisons. There are over seventy other correctional facilities like work camps, community centers, etc. At $47.83 per day per prisoner, Florida is spending 3 million dollars PER DAY for corrections. That's over 1.8 BILLION dollars per year! The cost to keep a man incarcerated ($17,500.00 per year) would be enough to send him to the finest university in our country and pay his room, board, and books and give him some extra spending money. Florida has more prisoners than most states, but the problem is similar in every state in the union. We've got a problem.

March - 1998

NORTH FLORIDA PRISONS

"This is always the worst part of your time down here: leaving!" That's what an inmate told me as we tore down my sound equipment at Jackson Correctional in northern Florida. We held services in four different prisons, along with five other ministry teams and almost one hundred volunteers who teamed up with Nelson Coblentz to blitz the northern Florida area. We were at Apalachee East and West, Jackson Correctional, and Liberty Correctional in a four-day period. We saw some friends that we had met in January with We Care and we saw many prisoners make commitments to Christ.

AUGUSTA COUNTY VIRGINIA ENCOUNTER '98

I am writing this letter from my motel room in Staunton, VA: birthplace of Woodrow Wilson, home of the Statler Brothers quartet, site of Civil War battles, and the center of much history of the United States. This is the site of Encounter '98, where Steve Wingfield is preaching every night about ten miles east of here. I am going into prisons and jails and several high schools every day as part of Encounter. It was a great week!

NEW VAN

At our February Common Ground Ministries board meeting it was decided that our '89 Ford van with 180,000 miles was probably due to be replaced. Before we could think how God was going to work things out, a friend donated his '95 Chevy conversion van with 25,000 miles to our ministry! So now, we not only have a newer, dependable van for family and volunteers, but we have a new confidence that God is going to meet our needs in every way. PTL! God is Good!

May - 1998

COLUMBIA CORRECTIONAL, PORTAGE, WISCONSIN

"Do you believe that in all things God works for the good to those who love God and are called according to His purpose?" The prison congregation shouted, "Amen!" Then chaplain Gene Dawson told this story:

> In February 1970, my barn burned down in Ohio. It was a huge 100' X 80' bank barn. It ruined me financially and I have never recovered to this day. But because of that fire, I met a young man who built pole barns and we have kept in touch over these twenty-eight years and he is the one who just presented Jesus Christ to you.

The applause was muffled, almost quiet, but genuine and from the heart. Columbia Correctional has the tightest security of the several hundred prisons I visited in the last nine years. We held two chapel services, each with forty prisoners and eight guards (including the chaplain). The guards were stationed in a circle around the men. Ex-farmer Gene Dawson is the chaplain in this maximum security prison, the prison where Jeffery Dahmer was imprisoned until he was murdered by two other inmates.

In this stifling, high security atmosphere, we presented the claims of Jesus Christ through song, and although the men were not allowed to even stand in response to an invitation (I was not allowed to take even my guitar into the prison), Gene assured me that His Spirit had been present and His word will not return void. As the men filed out without speaking, a quiet "Thank you" or "God Bless You" could be heard as they shook my hand. Maybe a murderer will be in Heaven because of a tragic barn fire.

MOBERLY CORRECTIONAL, MOBERLY, MISSOURI

Jack Murphy plays the violin on my recording of "The Touch of the Master's Hand." When I sing that song in prison I always tell of how "Murf" wasted his talented life until he met Jesus Christ. Among other crimes, he pulled off the biggest jewel robbery in American history and spent twenty years in prison. Then I sing the song accompanied by Jack's violin on the soundtrack, and I remind the men that "Therefore if any man be in Christ, he is a new creature; old things are passed away; behold all things are new" (2 Corinthians 5:17). It never fails to touch hearts in prison. But I wasn't ready for the response of one of the inmates in Missouri. He told me after the service that what I said about Murphy's robbery at the New York Museum of Natural History was accurate. "I know because I worked at the museum at the time. We were shocked, stunned, and insulted that Jack robbed us." He paused after telling me some more details and said, "I never thought I would follow in his footsteps!" The chaplain told me that this inmate has a Ph.D. in archeology and speaks five languages. He is a brilliant man. "If education were the answer, God would have sent an educator... but we needed forgiveness... so He sent a Saviour."

June - 1998

NEW SUPPORTER

WE'VE MOVED!

From Mt Hope to Walnut Creek! We have outgrown our little office in the former Mt Hope post office and have moved to the upstairs office space of the new Walnut Creek Cheese warehouse. Owner Mark Coblentz has offered us this space for three years at a rate well below market value. Thank you Mark and Walnut Creek Cheese!

NEW SUPPORTER

For the last three years, we have had a very comfortable financial margin. What a pleasure to not have to mention our financial needs in this monthly letter or in public meetings because of your generosity. Many of you have been supporting us for years and I wish I could thank each one of you publicly by name. Space does not allow that, but I do want to tell you about one unusual new supporter. Here is an excerpt of his letter:

Greetings John Schmid;

As I had mentioned to you earlier, I have been looking for a ministry and a missionary team I could support. I will be making small donations like this one to you, God willing, throughout the year. What I am able to give to your ministry I will also match, God willing, for Carl and Joann [missionaries to India]. Thank you for bringing them along on your last visit. Had it not been for groups such as Gospel Echoes, Gospel Express, and Common Ground Ministries, God's word may never have taken root in this young Christian. I thank God for the life-changing power of the Gospel...

This letter was signed by a man I recognized as an inmate we had met in prison, and a small check was issued by the prison from the Inmates Personal Fund. As far as I know, this is our first support from inside the walls of prison. How refreshing to receive from someone who has been a taker all of his life. I believe God will bless him because of his generous, regenerated heart.

ADAM SCHMID

Hello everybody! Today my baseball season ended. It was fun. I missed a lot of games because we travel so much. But the travel was fun, too (but not as fun as baseball). We have some more camps this summer, and Dad is going to some prisons.

LOOKING BACK

What a great July! It started out with a July 4 family reunion and ended up at a Wesleyan camp meeting in Houghton, NY. In between were prisons, churches, picnics, an office move, recording, and lots of summer things around home.

August - 1998

HOW TO BE HAPPY

Blessed (Happy) *are those who hunger and thirst for righteousness, for they will be filled.* (Matthew 5:6 NIV)

There is a thirst that is common to the heart of man, whether he be a preacher or a prisoner, a prince or a pauper. That is the thirst to be happy. And yet Jesus does not say, "Blessed are those who thirst for happiness," but, "Blessed are those who hunger and thirst for righteousness." Happiness is a by-product. It is the result of living a life of service, a life which pleases God and serves other people. Those who pursue only happiness are always unsatisfied. It is not something you find, but something that finds you! Here is the equation:

Seek Happiness = Nothing

Hunger & Thirst for Righteousness = Everything

We seek happiness, money, recognition, position, etc. These are all legitimate goals. But to obtain true happiness (blessedness) we must seek a higher goal, one that no one can block. That goal: to please God. Then "all these things will be added unto you." What happens to the person who hungers and thirsts for righteousness? He will be filled. Make righteousness your goal and you will be eternally satisfied (happy).

Can you believe that going into prisons makes me happy? Not so much that prisons are fun places to be, but when you're doing what God called you to do and thirsting after His righteousness, even prisons make you happy! Jesus didn't command us to hunger and thirst after righteousness; He only said that those who do so will be filled (truly happy).

IN THE CANADIAN PRISONS
by Ken Wengerd

"That will get you one of these!" an inmate said as he shoved his fist into my face. You never know how people will respond to what you say. We had been told that this section of the prison here in Canada was unpredictable because it was the medication unit and I was beginning to agree.

I was traveling through Canada with Glendon Bender and the Gospel Echoes Harvest team for a week of training, learning, instruction, and stretching, and as I stared at the balled up fist, I wondered, "Is this for me? Does God expect me to face fists?" And then I remembered Paul in prison and the encouragement he shared, and I was invigorated to carry the gospel in spite of fists in my face. The statutes of the Lord actually DO revive the soul. Psalms 19:7 (By the way, the man calmed down. He was just full of medication and had a different way of expressing himself.)

September - 1998

A VISIT TO LUCASVILLE PRISON

On Sunday, September 27, 1998, we went to Lucasville Prison for the first time in our ministry and the first time since the April 1993 riot where six inmates and a guard were killed. We had to leave home at 3:00 am to arrive on time for our three morning services (no more than 40 inmates at any gathering). The first two services were good times of worship, singing, and teaching. Six or eight homosexuals who attended for reasons other than worship attended the third service. We proclaimed the gospel and we are assured that God's word will not return void, but what a difficult atmosphere! It is so much easier to proclaim the Truth when the audience is on your side. At least we had the open door to have chapel service there. Pray for Lucasville.

MUSIC MINISTRY REACHES BEHIND PRISONS WALLS

On July 12, 1998, a group came in here at London. A lot of guys got saved that day. After church, I started to listen to your tape you sent, Everybody Needs Jesus. I played it over and over. After the lights went out in here I played the same tape again. I started to get cold chills all over my body. I knew what it was. It was Jesus knocking on my door, waiting for me to let him in. I prayed right then and I felt like I never felt before. The next morning I went to talk to the chaplain to help me to ask Jesus in my heart. I felt great ever since. I don't worry about these small problems anymore. I feel that your tape was what I needed to boost me to God, and I wanted to thank you very much...

– HOWARD
an inmate at London Correctional

MUSIC MINISTRY REACHES ACROSS THE OCEAN

I'm sure you will wonder who I am. I am from Northern Ireland. I used to listen in on your lovely radio programme every morning when I lived in Canada. I am 76 years old and I was happy to receive your tape. Your singing is beautiful... I sure do miss your inspiring messages every morning...

-IRENE BENNETT
County Armagh, Northern Ireland

(She thinks I am Chaplain Ray, but it was at least encouraging to know that our music reaches across the ocean.)

October - 1998

ARE TATTOOS A SIN?

You hear all kinds of questions in prison. I was talking with Sean at the Delaware Correctional Center near Smyrna, DE, when he asked if tattoos were a sin. Only a few prisoners do not have tattoos, so this subject has come up before and to my surprise, I found that Scripture does have something to say about it: "Do not... put tattoo marks on yourselves. I am the Lord" (Leviticus 19:28 NIV). I showed Sean what the Word of God said and I explained that even if it was sin, it is like every other sin in that Jesus died to cleanse us from it. Then Sean said, "Ever since I got this tattoo of the Grim Reaper, things seem to have gone downhill." He went on to tell of one failure after another until he eventually lost his wife and now he is in prison for failure to pay child support. "And it all seemed to start after I got this tattoo. What should I do?"

What would you have told Sean? He seemed so sincere and convinced that the tattoo had much to do with his bad fortune. Since I didn't know what to tell him, I reverted back to a basic premise: "The Main Thing Is to Keep The Main Thing The

Main thing." And since the Main Thing is Jesus, I said, "Sean, the problem may not be so much what's on your arm but what is lacking in your heart." Then I read the plan of salvation from the little booklet we were carrying and Sean prayed to receive Christ into his heart. Then I prayed with Sean that if the tattoo was really causing any problems, that God would break that curse and give Sean victory in Jesus. When we left the prison yard, Sean was smiling and waving good-bye.

We were in three different prisons with Nelson Coblentz in Smyna and Wilmington, DE, the week of October 20-22, and spoke with hundreds of prisoners every day and then held chapel services in the evening. Many prisoners made commitments to Christ. Pray for Sean and many like him who have accepted Jesus, but have never had patterns of success in their lives. It will be easy for Satan to convince these men that this won't last; that they are failures. Let's pray for victory for them!

WE CARE/CGM PRISON SEMINAR

"I did not know it could be so good," was one of the many comments about the Training For Effectiveness Seminar held this last month. We were challenged by We Care workers Jim Britnell and Steve Longenecker to continue seeking a relationship with the Lord. We were also given basic growth principles for doing any kind of ministry. These principles helped us realize that anyone can do ministry and that we are all called to do some kind of work for the Lord.

Another person said that the tools he received from the seminar were practical and down to earth and were going to help keep him focused in the future. It was a great weekend of fellowship, fun, and learning.

November - 1998

GIVE, GIVE, GIVE

Christmas is not a myth, not a tradition, not a dream. It is a glorious reality. It is a time of joy. Bethlehem's manger crib became the link that bound a lost world to a loving God. From that manger came a Man who not only taught us a new way of life, but brought us into a new relationship with our Creator. Christmas means that God is interested in the affairs of people, that God loves us so much that He was willing to give His Son.

-BILLY GRAHAM

GIVE, GIVE, GIVE....

Bob Pierce went to a successful businessman to ask for financial assistance in one of World Vision's many projects. The businessman said, "Pierce, as far as I can see, all this Christianity stuff is just 'give, give, give!'" Pierce looked at the man and said, "Thank you, sir, for giving me the greatest definition of Christianity that I've ever heard! You're absolutely right! God gave His Son, His Son gave His life, we give our lives to Him... and on it goes. What a brilliant definition of Christianity!"

As we enter into this 1998 Christmas season, may we be reminded, as Bob Pierce was, of God's gift to the world as we think of what gifts to give to which family members and friends. In the frantic rush to shop, buy, exchange, etc., may we pause to remember the reason for the season: God gave His Son. And if you have not given your life to God through the gift of the Christ-child (who grew up and became the Savior) maybe this will be the year that you will give the greatest gift you can give (your life) and receive the greatest gift ever given (eternal life).

LET EARTH RECEIVE HER KING!

Merry Christmas from Common Ground Ministries!

December - 1998

BELMONT PRISON SEMINAR

Neither snow, nor sleet, nor a state mandate to close the prison yard kept us from the New Year's weekend *Self Acceptance From a Biblical Perspective* seminar at Belmont Correctional. Ken Wengerd and I met with fifteen volunteers at the St. Clairsville Holiday Inn on the evening of January 1—amidst all the football games—to plan the weekend. It was our first winter storm and snow was falling the whole weekend. We made it to the prison on time but had to wait for over an hour to enter. We found out later that not only was visibility so bad that the prison yard was closed, but the roads were at level 3, which means that all State employees were to be dismissed from work. The prison officials discussed and argued for a while and eventually bent the rules to allow us to hold our seminar since we were there and the weather was too bad to go back home. The other problem, the level 3 roads, was not known until later in the day, so that didn't enter into the mix.

The problems we encountered entering the prison are not unusual. When you enter Satan's turf, he will do anything to discourage you from following through, and we have seen some crazy things happen. Very seldom do things go smoothly on entering a prison, but very seldom do we get turned away. I believe that your prayers are what breaks up the enemy's plans. That is why you are such a vital part of this ministry! In war, the heavy artillery (tanks, cannons, etc.) shoots over the heads of the foot soldiers and scatters the enemy so that the soldiers can then go in and clean up. Your prayers are our heavy artillery. Without you, we would be walking into sure defeat, or, at best, we would be simply entertaining, but with the enemy scattered by prayer, we walk in and clean up. Keep praying!

The seminar was a blessing to the prisoners, the officers, and the volunteers. Even the chaplain was taking notes. The seminar deals with anger, love, self-acceptance, spiritual warfare, etc. It is good stuff for all of us, but it is especially adapted for the man in prison. We had three sessions at the main prison, including Sunday morning chapel, and then over to the camp for a Sunday afternoon and evening session. The chaplain summed up the general attitude when he asked, "When can you come back?" Many lives were challenged and changed, with about ten men making first time commitments to Christ.

February - 1999

COSTA RICA WORK/MISSION TRIP

"Our doors are always open to you," said Roberto to missionary Dan Bair after an eight-day stay in his house in Carbon de Talamanca in southeast Costa Rica. "But Roberto," protested Dan, "you don't have any doors in your house!" Roberto laughed and said, "Next time you come we will have doors!"

That was typical of the kind of relationship that was built in just under two weeks with these struggling Nicaraguan refugees who have settled in this southern jungle area of Costa Rica. We arrived on February 12 to a group of happy, stand-offish church members near the little village of *Carbon* (pronounced, "car BONE") who were waiting on a group of twelve gringos who were coming to help them build a church.

After working hard together in 90-degree heat, high humidity, and rain for six days, Mauro, the lay leader of the church, summed it up in the Friday night farewell service when he said, "When you came just eight days ago you were strangers, and we stood around a little suspicious; even nervous. Now we say good-bye to you with tears in our eyes because you are family. Your help will not be forgotten."

We started with a half-poured footer and then took the 30'x50' building up to the last course of block, just ready for the crown beam, a formed and poured course of cement all around the top course of block which ties everything together and strengthens the building. The rafters or trusses will be set on top of that beam. (They're still discussing which would be better.)

What a blessed time of hard work, sweaty, sore muscles, bugs, and even snakes and monkeys! (Yes, we could see monkeys playing in the trees from our work site!) And when it gets dark in the jungle during new moon, it gets DARK! There are no pole lights, city lights... nothing. Several nights we went to bed at 7:30 pm. The houses we stayed in were various stages of primitive. One actually had indoor plumbing, but the rest were wooden houses with cement floors and an outhouse on one side and a cold water shower on the other side.

The people, who were at first a little embarrassed to have us in their humble homes, warmed up to us when they made the startling discovery that these rich Americans were just ordinary folks. The man who had the most primitive dwelling (dirt floors, no stove, just open fire, hogs running through the house...) said to me, "Next time you come we hope you can stay with us." I said I'd be honored to stay with him. And meant it.

Part of the expense that each person raised for the trip was $100 for work funds and materials for the construction. Since a man from New York had already sent $1,000 down for materials for this project, we were able to leave our $1,200 with the local Christians to finish the crown beam, rafters, and roof.

Whatever they don't get finished between now and July will be finished a group of twenty-five young folks from Pleasant View Mennonite Church near Berlin who are going down on July 12, 1999. They have asked me to go with them to show them the 'ropes' and after thinking it over for about five seconds, I agreed to go with them. What a joy it will be to see the same Nicaraguan and Costa Rican brethren and be able to continue to be with them again and encourage them with our labor and love!

Someday when you have a lot of time, let me tell you some of
the benefits of short-term missions!

March - 1999

THE PURSUIT OF HAPPINESS

I spent thousands and thousands of dollars trying
to find happiness when I lived in Southern California. My parents are very wealthy. We had maids and
chauffeurs and all the things that go with wealth. I
had 'everything'. None of that made me happy. Now,
here I am in prison and the only thing I own is a Bible and a coffee cup... and I'm happy! I found Jesus
Christ here in prison, and finally, my search for happiness is over!

William was sharing this story with me after our chapel service at Mansfield Correctional last week. During the service
I had told the story of ex-convict Jack Murphy and then sang
the song Jack helped me record, "The Touch of the Master's
Hand." Afterward, we tell of all the crazy things he had tried
in his search for happiness... girls, surfing, drugs, the occult
(he had been a member of The Church of Satan in California).
He had destroyed his relationship with his parents, his friends,
and anybody else who got in his way. Now, as a committed
follower of Jesus Christ serving a long prison term, he not
only was at peace but little by little he was restoring his relationship with his parents and family as he shared his faith in
Christ with them through phone calls and letters.

I asked him if he would put his story in writing for me and he said it is already in tract form and he will send it to me, but I couldn't wait to tell you his story, so here it is.

When will we realize that true happiness can only come through a relationship with God the Father through His Son, Jesus Christ?

TALAMANCA LAND PROJECT

"What can we do to help Fermin?" I asked. Missionary Dave Sharp said about the only thing we can do is pray. Fermin works at the local banana plantation near Limon, Costa Rica, from 4:30 am to late afternoon six days a week for very low pay. He leaves his house at 3:30 each morning to walk to work. He was not able to help us on the Carbon church project in February because of his job. He lives in a dirt floor tin house behind the church and although he is a hard worker and honest, it would not be wise to simply give money to someone who has never had much, as easy as that would be for us to do.

The next day Dave said, "There is something that could be done." There are six acres for sale behind Fermin's house at the cost of $6,000. If we could buy that land and then sell it to Fermin, (even though he could probably never pay it off) he could plant his own.

April - 1999

UPDATE: I came home from that mission trip and the next Sunday, I ran my idea past fellow church member Ron Himes. "Do you think it would be a good idea to raise the money to buy two hectares (four acres) for Fermin so he could raise his own crops and not have to walk the miles to the banana plantation?" Ron said, "I'll give $2,000." Within a week, enough money was raised to buy Fermin his own farm, right near the church. We sent the money to missionary Dave Sharp. In two years (the time it took to get the banana trees producing), Fermin quit his job at the plantation and grew his own bananas.

A CROOKED AND PERVERSE GENERATION

There was a time in America when we trained our children to pray. The first scripture I ever memorized was in second grade, public school. The first time I ever read scripture in public was in 8th grade, public school. It was made illegal that year, but we didn't know it yet. Morning devotions were just part of a normal public school day when I was a student. As a non-church attender, I don't remember being offended. In fact, I'm trying to think of any ill-effects of this "offensive, cram-it-down-your-throat, force-your-views-on-em" style of religious dominance, and for the life of me, I can't think of one negative instance among my classmates. Today, in place of morning devotions there are metal detectors, safe sex classes, classes for pregnant students, drug abuse classes... and this very week in some local high schools there are policemen in the hallways for the students' safety. What happened?

Since 1962, when prayer was taken out of school—and God was removed from the Supreme Court—cheating, stealing, the drop out rate, violence, pregnancy, rape, shootings, and now even murder in schools have increased, while test scores, attendance, class behavior, respect, etc., have declined. Coincidence? Many scholars and experts don't see any correlation, and although I'm no expert, as a casual observer and participant in prison ministry, I find it interesting that the boys who committed the tragic murders in Colorado on Hitler's birthday were wearing swastikas and Nazi symbols on their clothes and nobody said a word to them.

Meanwhile, a student in Michigan was threatened with suspension for carrying a Bible, and in other high schools, students were told to go home and change their offensive T-shirts that had Christian slogans on them. Paul told the Philippians that this is a "crooked and perverse generation." Isaiah warned, "Woe to those who call evil good and good evil, who put darkness for light and light for darkness" (Isaiah 5:20 NIV).

I believe we are reaping the harvest of more than thirty-five years of government-sanctioned "non-praying." The further we get away from God, the more confused we get. We don't seem to know right from wrong. It is hard to turn a big ship around, but I want to be involved in trying. Common Ground Ministries will continue to proclaim Christ in prisons (better late than never), camps, churches, street fairs, wherever we are invited.

Henry Blackaby said, "If darkness prevails, we can't blame the darkness; there must be something wrong with the light." Friends, it is dark out there today, but we can't blame the darkness. We must let our lights shine so that they (people) may see our good deeds and glorify our Father in Heaven. When you turn away from God, you don't turn to nothing, you turn to anything. Don't give up! God is in control! Proclaim Him!

May - 1999

TEN PRISON SERVICES IN ONE WEEKEND

The weekend of May 14–16, 1999, was probably the most efficient use of Common Ground Ministries personnel and resources since we began in 1990. We were scheduled to be at a weekend seminar at Belmont Correctional in southern Ohio that weekend. After everything was set with the chaplain and the prison officials, I received an invitation to participate with Bill Glass in a Weekend of Champions at eight prisons near Louisville, KY. The usual procedure would have been to decline with disappointment, because to be with Bill Glass is a privilege and a great opportunity, but we were already committed. I was able to ask evangelist Ken Wengerd if he thought he could handle the seminar weekend by himself (I knew he could) and then accept Bill Glass's invitation.

BELMONT, OH. Ken started the weekend at the local Holiday Inn with an orientation on Friday night for the fifteen volunteers. After a good night's sleep, they went into the Belmont Correctional Camp with Glendon Bender's seminar entitled *Godly Leadership.* After singing by Blood Bought, Ken taught two morning sessions and then went over to the main prison for a chapel service. Saturday night was the concluding session for the day and then two sessions on Sunday. The chaplain said that although the attendance wasn't what he had hoped for, the cream of the crop was there. Volunteers, prisoners, and Ken were tired and happy on Sunday afternoon. God is working at Belmont.

Northpoint... Frankfort Correctional... Kentucky State Reformatory...

Kentucky Women's Prison... Blackburn Correctional... Luther Luckett...

A Bill Glass Weekend of Champions is always an exciting time with lots of hype, hoopla, rah-rah, attention-getting action which is designed to draw prisoners to the platform on the yard, where the gospel of Jesus Christ is presented, usually in the form of a testimony by a world champion athlete or an ex-convict who speaks prison language. On this particular weekend, I was paired up on Friday with Frank Thompson, an ex-bank robber who spent sixteen years in federal prisons, including Alcatraz, and became a Christian in the Atlanta Federal Prison.

On Saturday I sang and opened three programs for Sandy Fatow, an ex-heroin addict, ex-girlfriend of Jimi Hendrix, a girl whose first four boyfriends are either dead or in prison! And then on Sunday, I traveled with Tino Wallenda of the famous "Flying Wallendas," the tightrope walkers. In each of these programs (we were not allowed to call them services) the speaker would tell of his experience with Jesus and then inform the prisoners that there are "teammates" (counselors) in the crowd who are waiting to help them with information on how to get to know Jesus Christ. The teammates each had copies of the Four Spiritual Laws. As the teammates and inmates got together to talk and share, the speaker and I would head out to the next prison.

What a weekend of flurrying activity, fun with great teammates, and what a great harvest of souls! I don't have the numbers, but several hundred men and over a hundred women made commitments to Jesus Christ in this three-day Weekend of Champions!

June - 1999

NOT READY TO "GIVE IT ALL UP"

In the rest home area of the Kentucky State Reformatory, I saw a man with a makeshift, dirty, two-inch strip of cloth across his face, tied from ear to ear, sort of like eyeglasses. I was trying not to stare at him when it dawned on me that he wouldn't be aware of it anyway. As I looked closer, his face didn't seem to have a normal shape. I found out that he didn't have any eyes or nose! Volunteer Sandy Fatow talked to him in his room and asked what had happened. "I got shot in the face with a shotgun," he said. Sandy, who has been in prison work for years, asked him, "Were you on your way to church when this happened?" The man just laughed. Then Sandy led him through the Four Spiritual Laws and asked him if he would like to pray the prayer to invite Jesus into his heart. After a pause, he replied, "Naw, I don't think so." When Sandy asked why, he replied, "I'm just not ready to give it all up."

I was reminded of Frank Constantino who got the same answer from an inmate in solitary confinement in Florida several years ago. Frank looked around at the human waste, garbage, and vomit on the floor, and at the vulgarities written on the wall in human excrement. The smells of sewage were coming through the cold steel bars of the man's maximum-security cell, and then he said to the man with a life sentence, "Yeah, you've got a good point. Who would want to give all this up?"

Sound ridiculous? It ought to, because it is. And yet, when I look at my own life—which was outwardly fine and respectable—I realize that I did the same thing for twenty-three years. I was clinging to things that, in reality, were sewage and garbage (wood, hay, and stubble) and saying, "I'm just not ready to give it all up." When I did surrender to Christ, the words of the old hymn became real to me: "And the things of this world will grow strangely dim in the light of His glory and grace."

Working in prisons not only helps me see the result of faulty choices and dumb decisions in the lives of prisoners, but it is like a mirror of my own life. The foolishness of not wanting to give up a life of living in a prison "sewer" is actually not much different than my reluctance to give up the lifestyle I had before Christ, even though it was totally acceptable in our culture. As we see the speck in our neighbor's eye, may we be mindful of the beam in our own eye.

Update: As we left the hospital area of the Kentucky prison that day, we walked through a gathering of about twenty men on an outside porch. They had gone out there to smoke and talk. One of them commented on my guitar, so I took it out of the case and sang a couple of songs. Then Sandy began to give her testimony of a life of drug addiction and immorality and how God saved her and set her free. Then she invited any of these men to ask Jesus into their hearts and be free, and nine of them did, including our friend with no face! He finally gave it all up!

GRAFFITI

Where was God during the Columbine tragedy?
— A STUDENT

I wasn't allowed in.
— GOD

July - 1999

COMMON GROUND MINISTRIES MOTORHOME REPORT

It's been three years since you helped us purchase a 1996, 29-foot Jayco Motorhome. This letter is to update you on the situation and to let you know how much we appreciate your support.

MILEAGE: The motorhome now has 60,000 miles (more than twice around the world).

MAINTENANCE COSTS (except for lube & oil change, etc.): $0.00 We have had no problems!

CONDITION: Looks and runs like new! (It is stored inside the pole barn that was built with volunteer help.)

PROJECTED LIFE EXPECTATION: We were told that this unit used the way we use it would last for three years. It has done so well and has given us so few problems that we have no immediate plans to replace it.

This motorhome has been such a blessing to our family and the ministry and I wanted to thank you again for your generosity in helping us purchase it. What we do is hard work and I love it, but this motorhome has made it so much easier. In fact, there were several programs that we would not have been able to accept had it not been for the motorhome.

God is good. We thank Him every day for His blessings and His mercy, and we think of you every trip we take. May God continue to bless you and may your gift to us be multiplied and leveraged in the Kingdom of God. Pray for us.

THANK YOU!

FAME AND GREATNESS

I was standing in line at the Cleveland airport with twenty-five tickets in my hand when I got the feeling that people were taking pictures of me. When I looked at the cameras, I noticed that they were aimed at the man standing behind me. I looked around at this smiling, bashful man and I couldn't believe my eyes! It looked just like Manny Ramirez! I said, "Are you Manny Ramirez?" "Yea." He was on his way to Boston to play in the All-Star Game. We talked as we stood in line for what seemed to be about two minutes. I was told later that we were in line for twenty minutes, but it seemed so short as I had the privilege of talking with one of my baseball heroes as if we were old buddies. He was so friendly!

About a half hour later, my daughter Amy and I went to the Burger King there in the airport to eat before boarding our plane. As we paid the man at the cash register, he said, "You look familiar."

"I do?" I asked.

"Are you a musician?" he asked.

"Yes," I answered

"You play guitar?"

"Yes."

"In prisons?"

"Yes!" I said. He stuck out his hand.

"You came to our chapel when I was in prison!"

I told him how good it was to see him outside of the prison bars and I asked him how he was doing and he said, "Great!" He has been out of prison for three months now and he is working at Burger King as part of his halfway house duties as he prepares for reentry into society. I will give his friends greetings for him the next time I am at that prison.

UPDATE: I did give his greetings to the chapel and to the chaplain the next time I was a Belmont.

I thought nothing could top meeting the major league RBI leader and clean-up hitter for our beloved Indians, Manny Ramirez. As I sat on the plane, however I realized that I was more excited about meeting this ex-convict–whose life has been restored through Jesus Christ and was touched through our ministry–than I was about meeting Manny (and I was really excited about meeting him). Maybe in my old age (maturity), I am beginning to realize what is really important; the difference between fame and greatness, between the temporal and the eternal, between the fun game of baseball and the real game of LIFE.

P.S. Go Tribe!

The first weekend of this year we had a seminar at an Ohio prison. Between services, a guard opened up to Ken Wengerd that he had been considering suicide. Ken counseled him from God's Word to not give up. When he saw Ken last Sunday, here's what he said:

"HEY! I HAVEN'T KILLED MYSELF YET!"
By Ken Wengerd

That was the greeting I received from a guard as we entered the prison this weekend! It was a beautiful sunny Sunday afternoon, and we were on our way into prison to do a service. We were feeling good about the program we wanted to do, and we were laughing and talking as we walked toward the front gate. What this man said brought us up short. Not everyone was happy; not all people have a purpose and a reason to live. I realized on Sunday this man is desperate, searching for a reason to stay alive, and he saw something in me that he wanted, the joy of Jesus Christ, the will to live, the need to make a difference. He told me that he wanted to come up to our area and take me out to eat some day. We made small talk about farming and about hunting and we left him sitting at the table in the entryway as we went off to the service. Part way through the service he came and motioned for me to come out; he had a piece of paper with his name and phone number on it. He told me, "If you get down this way again, give me a call; I want to talk."

Prison is such a hard place, not only for those who are locked up, but also for those who work there. What made this guard want to talk to me? Several months earlier we had sat and talked as we were being processed into the institution. He asked me what I thought about suicide and the effects of taking one's own life. As I shared with him he said that he had never heard it put that way before. The reason I believe that he asked me was because he heard what I taught in the chapel service, and he observed how we related to the guards as we were processed into the institution.

As we live our lives let us be careful how we relate to those around us, because we might just save them by how we conduct ourselves. I am reminded of the words penned by the writer of Hebrews around AD 70 almost 2,000 years ago (and it is still relevant for today): "Make every effort to live in peace with everyone and to be holy, without holiness no one will see the Lord" (Hebrews 12:14 NIV). Live your life so that others may come to know the Christ that lives within you.

FROM THE MAILBAG

... on July 12, 1998, a group come in here at London. A lot of guys got saved that day. After church, I started to listen to your tape you sent me, "Everybody Needs Jesus." I played it over and over. After the lights went out in here I played the same tape again. I started to get cold chills all over my body. I knew what it was. It was Jesus knocking on my door, waiting for me to let Him in. I prayed right then and I felt like I never felt before. The next morning I went to talk to Chaplain Cahill to help me to ask Jesus in my heart. I felt great since... I felt your tape was what I needed to boost me to God and I want to thank you very much.

-HOWARD

September - 1999

ANOTHER DIVINE ENCOUNTER

During the chapel service at the Grant County Jail in Marion, IN, I casually mentioned that I had lived in Costa Rica. After the service one of the inmates told me that he had also lived in Costa Rica for several years, and he mentioned the town, which I vaguely remembered. "What is your name?" I asked. When he told me, I recognized his family name and told him that I had been to his parents' farm and even told him who his neighbors were! He was amazed—as I was—and so glad to see someone who sort of had a connection. He had made a commitment that night.

I was telling this story the next day to Pastor David Terhune of Parkview Wesleyan Church in Marion. He then told me of his divine encounter at the Grant County jail.

Here is his story...

... I was on my way up the elevator to the fifth-floor jail chapel wondering what I was going to speak about. Chaplain Brady had called me just one hour ago to fill in as speaker for someone who had canceled. For some reason I was reminded of a tragedy that had happened twenty years ago in this very county that I had just returned to. Four children were playing near a lake the week before Christmas (that's why I thought about it; this was December 21). Their mother had warned them not to go out on the ice because it had not been cold enough yet, but as children do, they wandered out on the lake and one of them broke through the ice. His brother tried to rescue him and he broke through, as did his sister. The only one left on shore was the seven-year-old brother who ran for help. When the rescuers came, it was too late; all three children had drowned. I officiated the saddest funeral of my life; three children, all of one family, the day before Christmas. If only they had heeded their mother's warning!

I told this story to the prisoners and made the comparison: you are in trouble now because you did not heed warning after warning. When are you going to listen? It's too late for those children, but it's not too late for you! You can still be rescued! Come to Jesus! He's reaching for you!

A good number raised their hands to make commitments to Christ. When the service was over one prisoner stayed on the back row with his head down, weeping. The guards were nudging him, but he continued weeping. The officer gave me a look that meant, "Come tell this man to go, or we will." I went over and sat next to him. The prisoner asked, "Are you the man who preached the funeral for those poor little children twenty years ago?" "Yes. I am." He raised his head up for the first time and looked at me. "I was that seven-year-old boy!"

By now I was weeping, the guards were weeping; one officer went over and looked out the window so it wouldn't be noticed that he was crying. I asked the prisoner, "What are you doing in here?" He said, "I got picked up for speeding today. The officer ran a check and said there is a warrant out for my arrest.

When I asked what for, he said it was for failure to pay child support. I've never been married. It's a mistake, but now I see that God wanted me to be here to hear a message from the man who preached the funeral of my sister and brothers. Does this mean I will get to see them again now that I've accepted Jesus as my Savior?" "You will see them again!" I replied.

Now I understood why God would have a volunteer cancel, why Chaplain Brady thought of calling me; why a mistake in the police computer system held an innocent man in jail; why this twenty-year-old tragedy came to my mind. God orchestrated all these events to create a divine appointment to help heal a wounded 27-year-old who saw his siblings drown when he was only seven years old.

Coincidence? No! A divine appointment.

October - 1999

FUNNY THINGS HAPPEN IN JAIL

You just never know what is going to happen in a prison service. This month at a jail in Abingdon, VA, I was speaking on John 18. Peter (the fisherman, not Zorro) took a swipe at Malchus with a sword and cut off his ear (the equivalent of a foul tip in baseball—he was aiming for his head). Jesus rebuked Peter and healed the ear.

As I was speaking, I was reminded of a thought that Dr. Dennis Kinlaw had ventured out loud one time while preaching on this chapter. Do you suppose that years later the high priest might have noticed the scar on his servant's ear and said, "Malchus, what happened to your ear?" As I said this, I looked right at a prisoner to illustrate how the high priest might have examined the scarred ear with curiosity. The prisoner looked shocked and his eyes got big and everybody in the cell began to laugh. This was not meant to be humorous, so I was confused. Then I noticed it! The prisoner's ear was half cut off! He gave me a silly smile and then just laughed along with everyone else! In spite of (or maybe because of) that little coincidence, several men—not including our "ear" friend—made commitments to Jesus that morning. I wonder if that prisoner will think of Malchus and the healing power of Jesus the next time someone asks him what happened to his ear.

PRISON WORKER'S SEMINAR A SUCCESS

Actually, it wasn't just a prison worker's seminar, it was a Christian worker's seminar called *Training for Effectiveness*. For the second year in a row, Ken Wengerd organized and facilitated [that means he did all the work] a weekend seminar to help Christians be more effective in their walk and work for the Lord. Jim Britnell and Steve Longenecker, both prison workers associated with We Care Prison Ministries in Atmore, AL, along with Ken and I, were the speakers.

Steve is a pastor and a prison chaplain and Jim is an ex-convict with a dynamic prison ministry in Florida. Nine people participated in the two days of teaching at Pleasant View Mennonite Church and left with new tools and greater enthusiasm to share the love of Christ with everyone, especially prisoners.

Ray Hochstetler said, "I came because it was so good last year. I wouldn't have missed it for anything! I was so encouraged."

TEN YEARS OF COMMON GROUND MINISTRIES!

It's been ten years! We started on January 1, 1990, and God and you have faithful to us for all those years. We will tell you more in our January newsletter. Stay tuned. Thank you for your support.

November - 1999

CHRISTMAS IN JAIL

I asked a friend to tell me what it's like to be in prison during Christmas. Here is his response:

Dear John,

As I started reflecting back over the past seven years, I quickly remembered 1992, my first Christmas in prison, when almost any reminder of the season would bring tears of sadness and heartache to my life. Attending church services was especially hard, and I found it impossible to sing Christmas Carols without becoming choked up. The one thing that helped me through that first Christmas was the many holiday greetings I received.

December is probably the toughest time for us in prison, as we deal with pleasant memories from past holidays and dream of wanting to be with our family and friends. Tension increases, leading to more problems, additional stress, and a greater need to stay focused and acutely aware of what is happening around you.

As I prepare for my eighth Christmas here I can embrace it with enthusiasm and anticipation. Yes, I'll still greatly miss spending the holidays with family and friends. Yes, the tension will increase, and yes, it will be another Christmas spent separated from my sons. But yet, I will be celebrating the birth of my Savior, will be again blessed by holiday greetings, and will greatly enjoy the Christmas Carols and special programs at church. And the tears of my heart will now be of joy and gratitude for all that God has done for me through the birth of His Son, Jesus Christ!

- J.M.

TEN YEARS OF SINGING & PRISON MINISTRY!

August 1989 was my last month as a youth pastor. I was officially unemployed, starting to talk to many of you about the idea of a singing ministry. In a very short time, a board was formed, support was raised, and by January 1, 1990, I was able to quit my temporary job as a plumber (ditch digger) and concentrate full time on ministry. Over the years our focus has developed to this order of priority:

- Prisons
- Church meetings
- Camps
- Banquets
- Anywhere else

This year I was gone 144 days. By the end of the year, I will have had 230 programs, 75 of them in prisons, not counting the services conducted by my friend Ken Wengerd. Approximately 200 people have made decisions through these meetings. We can do this because of your support. God is good. He and you have been faithful! Thank you! May your last Christmas of this thousand years be your best!

Merry Christmas!!

JANUARY 2000

AD 2000! AD 2000! AD 2000! AD 2000! AD 2000!

A NEW YEAR!

A NEW DECADE!

A NEW CENTURY!

A NEW MILLENNIUM!

What a momentous time to be alive! Only twice since Jesus walked on this Earth have people had the chance to celebrate the beginning of a millennium! Our lives are marked off in seconds, minutes, hours, days, weeks, fortnights (two weeks), months, years, decades, centuries, and millenniums... I am beginning to believe that God wants us to use these units of time to look back and evaluate our lives, to remember what happened and give Him praise, and to learn from our mistakes and correct our course.

On the first page of the Bible God said, "Let there be lights in the expanse of the heavens to separate the day from the night and **let them serve as signs to mark seasons and days and years...**" (Genesis 1:14 ᴇꜱᴠ Emphasis mine). As we approach a new thousand-year period, let's look at a few major marks of past days and years:

- *One year ago* (January 1, 1999) I was planning a year of prison services, camps, concerts, etc.

- *Ten years ago* (January 1, 1989) marked the beginning of Common Ground Ministries; we were just trying to figure out what God had in store for us. Our third child was born.

- *One hundred years ago* (January 1,1899) my relatives were farming with horses, cooking with wood stoves and reading by coal oil lamps. None of them ever flew in an airplane—my Dad still hasn't.

- *One thousand years ago* (January 1, 999) after the Y1K panic was over, my ancestors were somewhere in Europe watching as the Crusades began marching across Europe to try to liberate Jerusalem from the pagans. Ironically, one thousand years later an attempt is being made to liberate the pagans from God!

In my lifetime, God has gone from being the One to whom we looked at the beginning of each school day to an illegal intruder who goes around offending people in the hallowed halls of tolerance and diversity. Just as the Crusades were ill-advised and not conducted with pure hearts, so the attempt to oust God from our society will ultimately fail. "No weapon that's fashioned against you (the Christian) shall succeed" (Isaiah 54:17 ESV).

What will we see one year from now? Ten Years? One hundred years? One thousand years? Revival? Ruin? Return? I am not one to predict the coming of Jesus, but I am among those who believe that His coming is imminent and could very well be today. No matter how we mark the seasons of time, we should be ready for His return. Martin Luther said we should live as if He were crucified yesterday, rose from the dead today, and is coming tomorrow.

HAPPY MILLENNIUM!

January - 2000

A GOOD STORY

Every now and then I hear a story that's so good, you've just got to hear it. This is one of them. Don't look for a deep spiritual lesson; it's just one of those fascinating prison stories of a man who had nothing to lose. I heard it at the maximum security Holman Prison in Alabama during the We Care Prison Revival in January.

After a comment about farming by a volunteer, Miguel said, "I used to grow my own food." The volunteer asked, "Were you a farmer, too?"

"No," said Miguel. "I lived in the woods for nine months."

"Was it a camping ministry?"

Miguel said, "No. I escaped from prison and I was hiding out."

"Oh."

The volunteer didn't know what to say, but I sure did. I went over to Miguel and asked, "How did you escape from this place?" Miguel went on to tell his wild story (in my words here):

He was stabbed with an ice pick nine times in prison and taken to the hospital. The pick went clear through his chest and out the back. His lung was punctured and he had lost a lot of blood. They pumped his lung back up and then Miguel had a heart attack on the operating table and died. He was pronounced dead; the prison was notified and he was wheeled out into the hall to be picked up by the morgue workers.

Miguel came to in the hall. He pulled the sheet off his head, looked around, and didn't see anybody. He said to himself, "I'm outta here!" and he walked out! For three days the Birmingham police were looking for his body because they knew his body had either been stolen or he escaped and would die soon. Miguel patched up his other wounds and started hitchhiking. He got a ride with an Alabama trooper to the state line and from there went to Montana where he camped in the woods for nine months.

When he thought things had cooled off he started going to town and eventually began to repair bicycles for a children's charity. He was so good and so well liked that they commissioned him to represent their organization in a cross-country bicycle ride. So with the charity's blessing and police escort through many towns, Miguel (or whatever his name was at this time) peddled for charity to the West coast and back.

He worked with the YMCA helping children. Everyone in town knew him. He had to work for cash only because he was dead. Then one day as he was on his way home on his bicycle, he heard his name on the police scanner that he carried everywhere with him. He had been featured the night before on the TV show, America's Most Wanted! Since everybody in town knew him, the police got dozens of calls. Miguel didn't go home that night. He hid out for ten days trying to get out of town, but the roads were all blocked and he began to realize that his escapade was over. "I turned myself in," Miguel told me with a smile. He had the look and tone of voice of a man who was talking about the semi-final game that he lost, but he had given it his best shot. As all escapees are, Miguel is now a hero in prison. He beat the system.

A highlight of our conversation was that Miguel said he is now a Christian. I didn't have time to ask details, so that story will be on page two! Have you ever heard such a story?

February - 2000

WEAVER LEATHER IN PRISON MINISTRY

About two years ago Paul Weaver, president of Weaver Leather, asked me to talk with Denise Benson in customer service. She wanted to know; wasn't there something they could do, with all the leather orders that get sent to prisons, to help the prisoners? One of the ideas that came up was to put a gospel tract in every order. Denise and Paul selected several different tracts that give the message of the gospel and began placing them in each prison order. Here is an excerpt from one of the many letters she has received in the last two years:

Dear Denise;

The other day I was going through a package from Weaver and I discovered the track that was placed inside—after looking it over I saw your name on it and the first thought was, Matthew 25:36 "...I was in prison and you came to visit me." Praise God!

The package I found your track in belongs to a guy that I help in the craft shop. He isn't a Christian and doesn't care to hear about God. There are many in the craft shop here that doesn't know Jesus, so please continue to send tracks in your packages, the devil has a stronghold here but we can claim victory for we hold the keys of the Kingdom of God (Matthew 16:19).

I guess I tell you this, that if it wasn't for servants like you trying to reach the unsaved in prison, I may not know our Heavenly Father in a personal way that I do. I thank you for doing God's work. I will be praying for you, Denise and Weaver, for your ministry through the mail by sending tracks.

In Jesus' Name,
Chris,
Amarillo, Texas

On a good day, ten percent of the prison population will come to a chapel service. But up to fifty percent will work in the prison leather shop during their time. Paul Weaver had already been involved in prison ministry through his prayer and financial support of our ministry, but now through the simple act of putting a gospel tract in each order, he and Denise are directly involved in reaching prisoners that otherwise may never come to chapel. Great job, Denise and Weaver Leather!

"I was in prison and you visited me."

WHAT HAPPENED IN MARCH?
(OR, I CAN'T THINK OF A GOOD STORY THIS MONTH)

March came in like a lion and went out like a lion. At least schedule-wise. I'm not sure how the weather was. Our January two-week family vacation/ministry trip in Florida changed into two quick trips to Florida (once with Lydia, and once with Adam) because of the last minute decision last August to send our children to school this year instead of homeschooling. That decision has turned our lives upside down because we can't just pick up and travel anytime we want, but they all love school and we are adjusting.

The second week of March I was involved in a prison ministry banquet in Marion, IN, with Jack Murphy and then to Olney, IL, to speak about prison ministry at a local church. A prison is being built in their community and they want to be ready to minister! What a vision that church has! We could all learn from them! From there I went to Sumter, SC, to be in several churches, including the church pastored by Ron Richardson, son of Bobby Richardson, former second baseman for the New York Yankees. What a thrill to play golf with a former Major League All-Star who still holds World Series records after forty years (even if he was a Yankee), but more than that, Bobby is a Major League Christian and treated me like one of his old friends. In my desire to go to the "least of these," God has allowed me to meet some of the choice servants in His kingdom.

CENTER OF GOD'S WILL: SECURITY, SAFETY, FULFILLMENT, JOY, HAPPINESS...

As busy as this year looks to be, I hope you don't ever get the idea that my work is drudgery. Many friends and supporters tell me, "Boy, prison ministry, I couldn't do it." Well, it is hard work and tedious and there are many disappointments working with prisoners and the government with all the scheduling and paperwork requirements, but what a joy when you know you're doing what you were created to do and you're in the center of God's will and lives are changed. I love it! I seem to fit in perfectly. In the words of my friend and colleague Steve Wingfield: "I have to pinch myself. How can God let me do what I love to do and allow me to make a living doing it?" I ask myself that question often.

My prayer is that you will find that niche that God has for you; that job that nobody else wants to do, but it fits you like a glove; that work that gets you out of bed in the morning and keeps you excited all day, even through the problems and disappointments and setbacks. The safest place in the world is in the center of God's will. Daniel was safer in the lion's den than were the guards on the outside because he was in the center of God's will. The three Hebrew children were safer in the fiery furnace, because they were in the center of God's will, than the guards were on the outside. I feel safer (and more fulfilled) in prisons and small churches, etc., than I would in a more secure secular job because I believe I am in the center of God's will. I continually remind myself what I preach and teach: There is no security in this world. Our only security is in Jesus Christ. The sooner we grasp that truth, the happier we will be.

April - 2000

PRISONERS

WE WANT THEM TO HAVE SELF-WORTH
So we destroy their self-worth.

WE WANT THEM TO BE RESPONSIBLE
So we take away all responsibilities.

WE WANT THEM TO BE A PART OF OUR COMMUNITY
So we isolate them from our community.

WE WANT THEM TO BE POSITIVE AND CONSTRUCTIVE
So we degrade them and make them useless.

WE WANT THEM TO BE TRUSTWORTHY
So we put them where there is no trust.

WE WANT THEM TO BE NONVIOLENT
So we put them where violence is all around them.

WE WANT THEM TO BE KIND AND LOVING PEOPLE
So we subject them to hatred and cruelty.

WE WANT THEM TO QUIT BEING THE TOUGH GUY
So we put them where the tough guy is respected.

WE WANT THEM TO QUIT HANGING AROUND LOSERS
So we put all the 'losers' in the state under one roof.

WE WANT THEM TO QUIT EXPLOITING US
So we put them where they exploit each other.

WE WANT THEM TO TAKE CONTROL OF THEIR LIVES,
OWN THEIR PROBLEMS, AND QUIT BEING A PARASITE
So we make them totally dependent on us.

From: Making it right: A Common Sense Approach to Criminal Justice by Dennis A. Challeen.
Melius & Peterson Publishing Corp. pp. 37-39

May - 2000

A DEATH BRINGS NEW BIRTH

"Do you realize what happened last night?" asked John. We were walking through the Delaware State Prison on May 10 as guest volunteers with the Gospel Express Prison Team. I remembered John because he had prayed the night before at the chapel service. He was a rough–looking man from South Philadelphia. With tears in his eyes, he shared his story:

James would not come to chapel. He was from a wealthy, prestigious Nashville music family and John had been telling him that Jesus could help him with the drug problem that got him in prison. He urged him to sign up to attend the special meetings this week. Each inmate had to sign up two weeks in advance in order to come to chapel; new rules. James was polite but firm; he didn't need religion. The night of our first chapel service, James got a death notice. His uncle had died. In prison, all death notices are handled by the chaplain, so James came to the chapel to call home, but all lines were busy. As he sat in the chaplain's office he could hear the music. The chaplain asked, "Would you like to stay for chapel while you're waiting to call?" James indicated that since the music wasn't all that bad and it was sort of his style (country)... yea, he would like to... but he hadn't signed up. The chaplain made a few calls to the front office and much to the surprise of both of them, permission was granted for him to stay. James came into the chapel; we sang and preached, and at the prayer of invitation, James came forward to commit his life to Jesus! Although I was the speaker at that service, I was unaware of this story until John told us.

This story not only touched and changed James—whom I never did meet—but inmate John was so elated that his rough-looking face was still glowing twelve hours later as we walked past his cell! Coincidence? No! Divine Encounter! God orchestrated a death in the family in such a way that victory was born out of tragedy. Pray for James.

June - 2000

YOU CAN'T ALWAYS BLAME YOUR BACKGROUND

We were waiting in the lobby of Lancaster Ohio Prison, Southeast Correctional, and I struck up a conversation with the officer on duty. How long have you worked here? Do you like it? What's the hardest part, etc.? In our casual conversation, he made an interesting observation: "The hardest part of my job is that I'm not allowed to be friends with the inmates. It's twice as hard for me because about half of my graduating class is in here." We laughed at his exaggeration, but the point was well taken. He had grown up with many of these inmates in the inner city of Columbus. "This also is an advantage," he said, "because they can't give me the old song and dance that they are in prison because of how disadvantaged they were.

Hey, man, I grew up in the same 'hood and I'm doing all right. You still got to make your own choices."

In my conversations with many inmates, I find myself vacillating between sympathy and disgust; between pity and a "you-deserve-it" attitude. When I hear an inmate's story, part of me always says, "No wonder you're in here. You didn't have a chance," and the other part of me wants to say, "Grow up and take responsibility for your life! I know folks who had it worse than you did and they're doing fine. Quit blaming everybody else for your stupid, sinful choices!" (I say this to myself, you understand.)

I'm not saying that your background and heritage are not important. The more sad stories I hear from inmates, the more I thank God for my parents and my upbringing, but no matter what your background, life is still a series of choices that you must make. The best environment ever created, the Garden of Eden, didn't prevent Adam from making a wrong choice, and one of the worst environments, forty days in the wilderness, did not persuade Jesus to choose wrong. Moses challenged Israel: "I have set before you life and death, blessings and curses. Now choose life, so that you and your children may live..."(Deuteronomy 30:19 NIV).

My friend Bob Moeller moved from pastoring an inner-city church in Chicago to an affluent church in the northern suburbs. When I visited him in June, he was saying that the contrast was amazing; from welfare recipients and street people to business owners and millionaires. "But one thing is the same," Bob said. "The problems. Whether they come to my counseling room on the bus or in their Mercedes, the problems are the same: 'How do I handle my teenager?' 'My husband is unfaithful.' 'I have cancer.' 'I don't have enough money and I'm unhappy.' 'I have all this money and I'm unhappy...' "

Rich or poor; inner city, farm, or palace; black or white; superpower or third world; the Bible has this message for us: "what may be known about God is plain to them... so that people are without excuse" (Romans 1:19-20). The message we present to inmates, church members, friends, or anyone who will listen is the same that Jesus proclaimed from the beginning of His ministry: "Repent ye, and believe the Gospel" (Mark 1:15). Modern psychiatrists would have us believe that it is not our fault. It's our parents, our environment, the umpire...

I challenge you as Moses did. Whatever your background, you are still in charge of the choices you make. Stop choosing to blame. Choose to be responsible. Choose life. Choose Christ!

July, August - 2000

NEWSLETTER FOUND!

If you happen to be one of those rare people who actually read all the mail you receive and are wondering where in the world the September Common Ground Ministries Newsletter got to, I have great news for you: This is it! I didn't send it out until now! Very seldom am I so busy that I don't get the newsletter out, because not only do I feel that I owe it to you who pray for us and support the ministry, but I enjoy keeping in touch and I enjoy the response and feedback you give.

But what a wild, crazy two months! Since I last wrote (August newsletter, sent out July 31) I have been in eleven states, three different countries, a week-long camp, a three-day retreat, fifteen prison services, a week-long evangelistic service, seven days of construction on our new office building here at home, and a Cleveland Indians game (they won). During the Canton, OH, Encounter 2000 week, I was also the speaker at Central Christian High School's "God at Work" week. So from Saturday, September 16, until Sunday the 24th (nine days), I spoke or sang at twenty-one services!

I am exhausted, excited, exhilarated, and ready to pound some nails here at the office-building project and spend time at the office. Hopefully, the population of Heaven has increased because of these efforts. We saw fruit in almost every service we were a part of; many prisoners came to the Lord; many decisions at the Canton Wingfield Encounter and even at Central Christian High School. students stood for Christ right in front of their peers, a courageous thing for a teen to do in our present culture.

SCATTERED FAMILY

During a five-day period in August our three children were in three different countries! Adam stayed behind in Costa Rica after a wonderful reunion of the English-speaking youth group I was a part of from 1981-83. I flew home for a family trip to Canada, but Amy stayed behind to attend volleyball camp. So our family time was Lydia, Katie, and me in Canada. Adam was in Costa Rica, Amy in the U.S., and Katie in Canada! We all got back together and everyone seemed happy, so maybe it was family time after all, but I remember as a child that just going to Wooster was a major family event. We live in exciting times!

NEW CGM OFFICE BUILDING COMPLEX

The Common Ground Ministries International Offices are relocating to a prime real estate location on the outskirts of Benton, OH. Okay, I'm building a barn in my yard to use as an office. That doesn't sound nearly as exciting, but the truth is, it's a major project for the ministry and me. The rafters are up and the general contractor (me) is getting ready to put the roof on.

In eleven years as a ministry we have been:

1. at home

2. in the basement of Dutchland Construction's log home

3. in Mt. Hope

4. upstairs at Walnut Creek Foods

5. and now, back home

September, October - 2000

THANKSGIVING:
AN ATTITUDE OF GRATITUDE

On December 4, 1619, a group of thirty-eight English settlers arrived at Berkeley Plantation on the James River near what is now Charles City, VA. The group's charter required that the day of arrival be observed yearly as a day of thanksgiving to God.

In 1789, President George Washington issued a general proclamation naming November 26 a day of national thanksgiving.

In 1863, Abraham Lincoln proclaimed the last Thursday in November of that year as "a day of thanksgiving and praise to our beneficent Father." Each year afterward, for seventy-five years, the President would formally proclaim that Thanksgiving Day should be celebrated on the last Thursday of November.

In 1939, Franklin D. Roosevelt changed Thanksgiving Day to the third Thursday in November to help businesses by lengthening the shopping period before Christmas.

Two years later, in 1941, Congress ruled that the fourth Thursday of November would be observed as Thanksgiving Day and would be a legal federal holiday.

We come from a heritage of gratitude. Our forefathers were grateful people who knew whom to thank for the blessings that were bestowed upon them. Every now and then our government does something right, and this Thanksgiving Day legislature is a prime example. Although you can't force a person to be thankful, it sure doesn't hurt to be reminded of how blessed we are. A national day of Thanksgiving can do that. These reminders are nothing new. When the children of Israel crossed the Jordan River, they piled up stones on the shore as a memorial to God's faithfulness. "In the future, when your children ask you, "What do these stones mean?" tell them that the flow of the Jordan was cut off..." (Joshua 4:6,7). I sometimes sing, *"Count your blessings, count them one by one... see what God has done."*

In this Thanksgiving season, are you thankful? Do you realize how much we have to be thankful for? I only have to take a short-term mission to anywhere else in the world to realize how lavishly God has poured out His blessings on this nation in general and on me and my family in particular. Every time

I come out of a prison, I realize how blessed I am. First of all, that I am free. Second, that I had, and still have, good parents. Third, that I have a good wife and wonderful children. Fourth, I have good health. Fifth, God has given me a place in service to Him. Sixth... I think you get the point. I am thankful. God is good.

In this Thanksgiving season, may we be thankful for His abundant blessings! May we use them to serve Him and make His name known!

HAPPY THANKSGIVING!!

November - 2000

MERRY CHRISTMAS!

"I've got good news and bad news for you," I told the prisoners. "Which do you want to hear first?" "Give us the bad news first," they all yelled.

For some reason, they always want the bad news first. Then I told them this story:

No matter how well you behave yourselves from here on out, there is one more judgment coming. That's the bad news. The good news is that the Judge in that final judgment is holy and righteous and good. But, there is more bad news: every one of us is guilty. And yet, guilty as I am, I have the assurance that I'm going to "walk" (go free). How can that be? When a guilty man goes free, someone had to do something illegal or immoral, or someone was paid off. But in that final judgment, none of that happens, and yet I go free. Explain.

Here's the story I tell to try to explain how God set a guilty man like me free:

TRUE STORY

A girl in California got stopped for speeding. She went to court. She pled guilty. The judge's gavel came down and he said, "Guilty. I hereby fine you $500." (Don't speed in California.) When everything was over, a very strange thing happened. The judge stood up, took off his black robe, and came around the bench. He reached into his pocket, pulled out his checkbook, and paid the girl's fine! Sound strange? (Usually, when I tell this story, you can see the perplexed look on prisoner's faces.) This really happened! Can you figure out why the judge would do such a thing? Here's one little fact that explains his action: The judge is the girl's daddy. He loves her. But while he is behind the bench, he is her judge, and since he is honest, as much as he loves her, he must punish her according to the law. But now, after court, in front of the bench, he is no longer her judge; he is her daddy. And he loves her so much that he wants to pay her fine. No one did anything dishonest, the law is satisfied, the fine is paid, the girl is free.

Do you get the connection? Especially in this season of the year, we see how God the judge looked down on us from the bench, and although He loves us, He must say, "Guilty! I hereby fine you... DEATH." But He loves us so much that He stood up, took off His judge's robe, came around the bench (into a manger, onto a cross, up from the grave) and paid our fine for us. No dishonesty, the Law is satisfied. I'm free!

MERRY CHRISTMAS!

December - 2000

AD 2001!

We thought that last year was the new millennium and now the experts are telling us that, "No, it's this year." All that worry last year for nothing! But I guess you know that the experts can be wrong.

In AD 252 the monk Dionysius Exiguus started a Christian system of dating events, beginning with the year that Christ was born. He counted back the years to the birth of Jesus and declared, "This is 252 anno Domini!" (in the year of our Lord). It was actually a very good idea, much simpler and more accurate than always saying, "In the third year of such and such a king." The only problem is that Dionysius was off by about four years. We know from secular history that Herod died in 2 BC and Jesus was born before Herod's death, some say about two years. Therefore, this is actually closer to AD 2005 than 2001, so the new millennium wasn't last year OR this year, it was four years ago, according to the records in Heaven! What I'm trying to say is: God is in control. Y2K didn't worry Him and even if it would have been as big as some prophets predicted, it shouldn't have worried us. With Isaac Watts, we can sing and shout with confidence:

> He rules the world with truth and grace
>
> And makes the nations prove
>
> The glories of His righteousness
>
> And wonders of His love...

SCHMID FAMILY SUMMARY, 2001:

Lydia: In December we celebrated twenty years of marriage. Lydia is my secretary two days a week and my best friend 24-7 (that means all the time). She keeps things together on the home front as well as helping the ministry with scheduling, volunteer coordination, and office managing, etc.

Adam: On January 18, it will be sixteen years since the birth of our first child, after four miscarriages. Adam is still our miracle baby. I thank God for him every day, even though he's no longer a baby, and it's a miracle if he does his work. Exactly two days after his 16th birthday he will take his driver's exam. I have to admit that I am almost as excited as he is. Adam is a sophomore at Central Christian High School in Kidron, Ohio.

Amy: An eighth-grader at Central Christian, Amy played volleyball this year. She is developing into a young lady. She enjoys reading and traveling and will be going with me to the Short-Term Missions Conference in Atlanta. She and Adam are in Mini-Term right now.

Katie: After a year at Berlin Elementary (5th grade), Katie transferred to Central. She misses her Berlin friends but has adjusted well. She is playing biddy ball this year. (That's 6th-grade basketball for those of you, who, like me, who never heard of such a term.)

John (me): I will quote my friend Steve Wingfield: "I have to pinch myself—I can't believe God would allow me to do exactly what I love to do and provide a living at the same time." God is good—all the time!

January - 2001

ARE YOU JESUS?

Prison ministry and short-term mission's teams have this in common: They not only bring hope, light, and salvation to those whom we visit, but the volunteers who take this good news are also blessed. This past month I was privileged to be a part of the annual We Care Prison Revival in Atmore, AL. Then I went to Florida to sing with The Inspirations in a Haiti missions benefit concert, and then to Atlanta to a short-term missions conference. Why do I do these things? Why go to prison, to other countries, to concerts...? I think it can be summed up in a story that a friend, Jim, told at the short term missions conference in Atlanta:

They were running through the marketplace in Mexico. People were pushing and shoving as they ran to catch their bus. In the confusion, someone brushed against a bushel basket of apples and they spilled all over the floor in the busy marketplace. Only a few noticed it. No one stopped. As Jim reached the bus stop, he could not get the spilled apples out of his mind. Some vendor was going to have to pick them all up. At the risk of missing his bus with all the American volunteers, he ran back and saw a young boy scrambling to gather all the apples. Jim got down on his hands and knees and helped the boy and then gave him $10 to pay for the bruised ones. The boy said "Thank you" and then yelled as Jim started to run back to the bus stop, "Hey mister!" Jim turned around. The boy said, "Are you Jesus?"

Jim never did tell us if he caught his bus, but I could tell by his excitement that it didn't matter. He had found the secret of missions, of prison ministry, of the normal Christian life: To be Jesus to those who have never met Him. I guess that's why I go to prisons, to other countries, to banquets, concerts, and churches: To be "Jesus" to someone who needs to see Him. "Let your light so shine before men, that they may see your good works and glorify your Father which is in Heaven" (Matthew 5:16). May we be Jesus to all we meet, overseas, in prisons, concerts, and most of all, at home.

NEW DRIVER IN BENTON

On the 26th of January, Adam took his driver's exam in Millersburg, passed with flying colors, and then drove back to Kidron all by himself. Just like that! In our culture, that's one of the rites of passage for a young boy to become a man. We spent the first two years of his life trying to get him to walk and talk, and the next fourteen years trying to get him to sit down and be quiet! And now, he just drives off into the sunset!

Actually, we are excited for him and trying to adjust to the fact that children grow up, our family is changing, and that this is normal. God has blessed us richly. Oh, yes! Amy and Katie are also excited. They now have a personal chauffeur, at least mornings, and don't have to ride the bus. Riding a school bus is so uncool. And they can sleep in for five more minutes!

February - 2001

KATIE MADE 'EM CRY...

Five years ago, we took our children with us to the We Care Prison Crusade in Atmore, AL. It is always a special time when the children can go into a prison with us because they seem to touch the heart of a prisoner in a special way. But even with the children along, the daily progress in ministry can't be measured like it can in construction or farming or other physical work, where one can look back and see how many blocks have been laid or how much land has been plowed. We're never sure if our service did any good or not. We work with the realization that sometimes only eternity will tell if anything happened. Every now and then, however, we receive a letter like this one:

Feb. 7, 2001
Dear Miss Katie Schmid;

I saw your Dad during the January 2001 We Care Crusade and I asked about you. I was at the Frank Lee Prison Crusade team when you came with your Dad about five years ago. I clearly remember that your Dad lifted you up on the tabletop and you both sang so beautifully, and concluded with, "Daddy, What If?" Many eyes of the hardened men, including my eyes, were weeping for the joy and beauty that you and your Dad gave us and to the Lord. So many men had young daughters like you and deeply missed seeing them, so your presence, which was so unafraid, was touching and appreciated, too!! May God bless & keep you...

Bill
Volunteer Chaplain

I remember that particular service at Frank Lee prison five years ago. It was Amy's ninth birthday, so Katie would have been six years old (the next day, Adam turned eleven in prison). When former Chaplain Bill told me what an impact Katie's song had on the men, I asked him if he wouldn't put that in writing so I could encourage my children that their singing actually makes a difference (sometimes they're not so sure). He ended up writing a personal letter to Katie. Thank you, Chaplain Bill. And thank you, Katie, Adam, and Amy for your willingness to be used by God through this ministry. It is such a blessing to me when we can sing together as a family. With all the activities that the children have now that they're in school, our opportunities to sing together as a family could be in jeopardy. We'll sing together when we can, and when they have school activities we'll support them there. God has been good to us!

March - 2001

LIFE IS SHORT

I attended four funerals in March. Let me tell you how each of these saints were a part of who I am.

Levi Gingerich, 84: I went to school with Levi's children. Son Jake and I shared the same seat in 8th-grade reading class because we had twenty-six students and thirteen books. Pat (Eli) and I worked on the same carpenter crew for four years, which is the era I learned to play guitar, mostly from Pat's instruction. During that time I practically lived at the Gingerich home, which is one of the reasons I can speak Pennsylvania Dutch today. Almost twenty years after Jake and I suffered through "The Courtship of Miles Standish," I married one of his cousins, so now we're family. When Jake's son was tragically killed in an accident, I was asked to preach at his funeral. Levi left a legacy of faithfulness to God, his family, and his church.

Elias Frey, 85: A hall of fame auctioneer and a faithful friend of the Mennonite Church, Little Eden Camp, Bill Glass Prison Ministries, Common Ground Ministries, and a multitude of other charities, Elias and his family became our good friends when we met at Little Eden Camp about ten years ago. It seems like we knew him all our lives. (I've known about his tractor auction since I was little.) He was always the life of the party at camp and his auction business was known around the world. Yet, with all the fame and fortune and the huge amount of money he gave to worthy causes, at his funeral I was most impressed by the testimonies of his children—he was first and foremost a father and a husband. He may have gained a good portion of the world's goods, but not to the neglect of his first responsibilities; his family and his church. What a heritage!

Mildred Gwin, 89: My fourth-grade teacher. Outside of my parents, probably no one influenced me as much as my teachers. I went on to high school, college, and then graduate school, which means I had a bunch of teachers in my time (and it also means I am over-educated), but only my high school football coach can rival Mrs. Gwin's influence in my life. I especially think of her every Christmas when I recite the Christmas story. I memorized it in fourth grade. She wrote the first twenty verses of Luke 2 on the blackboard and we would recite it. Then some lucky student would get to go up and erase one word, and we would recite it again. By Christmas break the board was empty and we recited the whole passage. I can still recite it after forty years. As someone mentioned at the funeral, when Mrs. Gwin taught at Franklin Township School, it was a parochial school! She taught for forty-two years with an average of twenty-five students each year. With her influence on these 1,050 lives, she can truly sing her favorite hymn, "O For a Thousand Tongues To Sing"!

Elaine Asfahl, 67: We worked with Elaine and Marv for seven years in Costa Rica, and I knew her before that because Marv came to Asbury College as a mission representative for WGM. Later, he was youth pastor at the Wilmore UM Church. Of these four saints, Elaine's death seems to be the most untimely. She was still in her prime and she and Marv were mentors to hundreds of young Latin youth as directors of Young Life International. As much as we hated to see her go, her memorial in Iowa was a celebration of a life well lived, a family well raised, a Godly heritage passed down, a family that grieves, and a hope that endures.

The older I get, the more I understand John Wayne's statement just before he died at age 76: "I never dreamed that life would be so short." I can still hear Rev. Paul Hummel say, "Only one life and soon 'tis past. Only what's done for Christ will last." Each of these dear friends was ready to go. Each of them left a heritage. Partly because of them, I have dedicated my life to helping as many as I can to get ready. Give your life to Christ; make your funeral celebrations like these were.

April - 2001

PRISONER GETS NEW PERSPECTIVE ON "A MESS OF POTTAGE"

I remember as a teenager in the 1950's, laughing at Esau for trading his inheritance for a "mess of pottage"—a bowl of vegetable soup! How silly that sounded! The family was rich, with herds and tents and many servants. Grandpa Abraham had been called a "prince" by townspeople who saw all he had.

Now, Father Isaac was leader and Esau and his twin, Jacob, were crown princes. True, they didn't attend fancy prep schools, and one liked to hunt and the other worked around the house, but they were the heirs.

How heedless could Esau be, when, after one unsuccessful hunt, he came in, famished but with nothing to cook, and asked for a bowl of soup. Jacob, always jealous as the younger son, knowing he only gets 1/3 of his dad's wealth, set an incredibly high price on his soup: the other 2/3. He may have laughed as if it were a joke. Esau agreed to trade his birthright, and the joke was over. As soon as the family heard, they held him to his word and he found he had stupidly, carelessly, given away all he would have inherited.

I remember thinking, "What a jerk!" As a younger son, I had never envied my older brother or worried that he'd inherit more than me. I couldn't understand such stupid gluttony, since obviously Esau wasn't really going to die of starvation.

Yes, I remember laughing at Esau, like it was yesterday. Then I committed a crime and landed in prison five years ago. A minister asked, "What did YOU sell your birthright for? Did you get a better deal than Esau did?"

My God—how stupid I'd been! How the tables were turned, and I saw myself, like Esau, discovering that tears and pleading wouldn't change society's judgment of my stupidity. That "mess of pottage" was the most expensive meal I'd ever eaten, just as it was for Esau. No amount of "exceedingly great and bitter" crying will change the past.

I remember my home and wife, my children and dogs, my business and hobbies, my joy at my work and the fun on vacations. And the Parole Board asks, "Do you regret committing your crime?" "Yes!" Then they say, "Due to the serious nature of your crime, it would make a mockery of the law to parole you at this time." So, they may ignore those printed guidelines, the ones the judge looked at when he said, "Fifteen years!"

Yes, I'll always remember Esau's folly at trading his inheritance for a mess of pottage—but I won't smugly laugh anymore.

-A.R., MISSOURI

An inmate friend of mine entered this testimony in an essay contest sponsored by the prison library. It is his story of a bad trade.

Professor John Oswalt said that one possible title for the Old Testament could be, *What Could Have Been: If My People Would Have Only Listened!* I suppose most of us could entitle our autobiographies the same way. The New Testament message is: What Can Still Be. What a hope! No matter how badly we've messed up, God can still make us what we were created to be. He can restore the years that the locusts have eaten. Don't trade your inheritance for a mess of pottage.

May - 2001

COMMON GROUND MINISTRY NEWS UPDATE, COSTA RICA TRIP

I got back last night, June 13, at 12:30 am from a thirteen-day work/mission trip to Costa Rica with twenty youth. I came back a day early because of a concert at the Amish Door Restaurant tomorrow at noon and 6:30 pm. I didn't want to risk a delay at the Houston airport, which would have gotten me home too late for the matinee part of the concert. The team was in good hands with leaders Wes and Betty Miller and Lee and Barbi Beachy. They are at the airport in Costa Rica at this very minute. With these miraculous little cell phones, I was able to just now call the bus driver and make sure that all is going well (it is). When we lived in Costa Rica just twenty years ago (just?), the only way to call to the States was by ham radio or a very expensive phone call. (We once called my parents in 1981 for ten minutes for $50.00!) Times have changed! The world is getting smaller.

The work project went well. Actually, it was rated somewhere between fantastic and terrific! We helped finish Sunday School rooms, put in a second floor, put on steel siding, painted, wired, tiled, etc., for Iglesia (church) Menonita de Barrio Jesus near the town of Heredia. When we left, we could look back and see what we built, and the local church members were very happy. But as important and helpful as the work was, the most important things that were built were the relationships with the people. We all stayed with local families, and even though there was a language barrier, there was no love barrier. Yes, there was somewhat of a food barrier, but when a man gets hungry enough, he will eat rice and beans. The first night in a Costa Rican home was scary for most of the team, but by the time we left, there were tears and hugs of good-by for their family.

I WAS IN PRISON WITH DIFFERENT MINISTRIES

I had the privilege to be in twelve different prisons in May with three different prison ministries. The first ten days of the month I was on a prison tour in Wisconsin and Missouri with our own Common Ground Ministries. One of the prisons I visited was Columbia Correctional in Portage, WI, where my longtime friend (and ex-farmer) Gene Dawson is the chaplain. This is the most secure, maximum security prison I have been in. It is where Jeffery Dahmer was incarcerated (and murdered). There were eight guards in each chapel service of 40 men, one guard for every five men! In spite of the stifling atmosphere, several men made commitments to Jesus.

On May 13, I went to Madison and London prisons in Ohio with the Freiheit Messengers, an Amish group from Sugarcreek, and as far as I know, the oldest prison ministry in Ohio. Two weeks later I was in the Kentucky State prisons with the Bill Glass Weekend of Champions and many professional athletes. What a difference in ministry styles and approach! Each of these ministries was very different but very effective in its own way, and prisoners came to Christ in each service.

June, July - 2001

A LETTER FROM PRISON

Dear John,

Is it really true that my days behind the walls of prison are few in number, and that this is probably the last letter I'll write you from here? The thought of getting out could easily become overwhelming, as the adjustments and issues will be many, and yet, God...! He'll continue to be with me, being my Protector, Provider, and Sustainer! I do not want to give the impression that I don't have some concerns and fears, because I do, and I know there will be many challenges and some real struggles.

For just a moment, imagine with me what I am about to face upon being released. For over 8-1/2 years I haven't rode in a vehicle, touched a tree, been in a store, ate an ice cream cone, or handled money. When I get out I have to get a driver's license, open a bank account, work a 'real job', and buy a million things. I'll see and talk to people I haven't seen since coming to prison, and be greeted and then live in a world that's changed so much. Yes, in many ways it will be like starting life over, though with the label of being an ex-con, with society's attitude towards offenders, and as a new creation in Jesus Christ. But God...! It's because of Him that I can embrace my tomorrows with anticipation and enthusiasm!

He wrote much more, but I wanted you to "read over my shoulder" these thoughts and fears of a man who wants to serve God and is about to get out. Pray for this man (let's call him "John"; God will know who you mean) that he will remain faithful and be able to re-enter society smoothly. Can you imagine the challenges that he will face?

FAMILY NEWS

On July 29, Adam and Amy were baptized into the faith! They sealed the commitments they made to Jesus when they were just five years old, and they continue to re-commit their lives and grow in the faith. I had the privilege of assisting pastors Scott Hochstedler and Ben Raber in the baptism. Lydia and I are excited and proud as we continue to pray that they will grow in the grace and the knowledge of our Lord and Savior Jesus Christ. Katie will join them in going back to Central Christian School on August 22 for the '01-02 school year. They are excited about school by a two-to-one vote.

August - 2001

LABOR (work)

The Labor Day weekend has just passed (yes, that means I didn't start writing this newsletter until the day it was supposed to be in your mailbox). Labor Day started around 1880 when a carpenter from New York City and a machinist from Paterson, NJ, began suggesting a holiday to honor the American working man. They helped stage the first Labor Day parade in New York City in 1882. Five years later, Oregon became the first state to legalize Labor Day as a holiday, and in 1894, president Grover Cleveland signed a bill making it a national holiday. Now we honor the American workforce by loafing all weekend.

For a while now, I have been thinking about "work." This Labor Day weekend I was part of an amazing display of what can happen when people work together. I went to a barn-raising. I saw an 84'x80' bank barn erected in less than eight hours! That's almost quicker than it took to burn it down when lightning struck it on August 9. When I had to leave at 11:00 am, before lunch, the roof and sides were 95 percent done! Here at home I just finished a 24'x36' barn (our international headquarters) in nine months!

The barn I helped raise on Saturday was more than ten times larger (when you consider volume and height) and it was completed in one day, compared to 270 days for mine! One small difference was that on Saturday there were close to 800 men working. I have been to a dozen or more barn raisings in my time because I used to work for a barn builder, but Saturday I was almost overwhelmed by what I saw. By 8:00 am the beams were all up, rafters were on and roofing was being handed up, while at the same time the siding was being put on. I was one of about twelve men helping put one section of floor down while another crew was doing the same coming from the south end. We met in the middle, sort of like the transcontinental railroad. When our little section of floor was done, I looked up and all 6,720 square feet of barn floor was done! So, we started on the grain bins...

The Bible says that work that's done for the Lord is not in vain. "The night is coming when no one can work" (John 9:4 NIV). Are you having a hard time with your job? Try thinking enthusiastically about it. Your job will become fun. You'll do a better work and you will put a touch of glory in your life. I love my job. Glory!

September - 2001

ATTACKED!

On September 11, 2001, our lives were changed forever. Like most of you, I will remember for the rest of my life where I was when I heard that the World Trade Center had been hit by hijacked airplanes, just as I still remember exactly where I was thirty-eight years ago when the High School principal's shaking, emotional voice came over the intercom system and said, "The president... of the United States... is dead."

These are called "defining moments." There have been several in my lifetime: President Kennedy; Martin Luther King; Bobby Kennedy; Man on the moon; Kent State; Elvis Presley; John Lennon... and now, the World Trade Center.

Nothing will ever be the same again. Our security has been shaken. Our economy has been hit. More than 6,000 people are dead or missing, which means that tens of thousands of families (children, spouses, parents) will never be the same. Joseph Stowell pointed out that if the funerals of every person who died in the hour of attack would be held one a day in succession, we would be attending a funeral every day for more than six years! Such grief and destruction is almost too much to comprehend. Even though I personally didn't know any of the victims, I realize it is an attack against me and my family, too.

What did the enemy attack? They aimed at the center of our finances, the World Trade Center, and they brought it down. They hit the Pentagon, the center of our military power, and it is wounded. But the foundations of these buildings are still intact. If the decision is made to rebuild, the same foundations can be used. They are solid. But as pastor Jerry Durham noted, our country was not built on financial power, nor by military might. We were vastly outnumbered by the most powerful empire in the world in 1775. America, with all her faults, was built on faith in Jesus Christ. Our forefathers prayed without shame in Congress. The building of our faith has been in shambles for years, but it appears that maybe the foundation is still there! For several weeks now Americans have been realizing what is really important. I would suggest to you that when the local store signs urge us to pray; when the local government officials urge us to pray; when the Governor of the state and the President of the United States and even the dominant liberal media urge us to pray—God is at work!

In the face of this terrible tragedy, I see God working. After all the shock and grieving and prayers for the families of the victims and fear of the future, I would like to suggest the following spiritual truths that seem to be more evident than ever:

- There is an enemy.

- The enemy is real.

- The enemy plays for keeps.

- The enemy doesn't play fair.

- The enemy will not be victorious in the end.

- There is no real security in this world.

- Our only security is in Jesus Christ.

- We do not have to fear. (The phrase "fear not" is found 365 times in the Bible.)

- Jesus is the answer.

- Be ready.

October - 2001

OCTOBER REPORT

The month of October offered us ministry opportunities as varied and different as Columbus Day is from Halloween. I had the privilege to be at the wedding of Michelle Wingfield in a beautiful Presbyterian church in Virginia, and then the unusual honor to preach at the Amish funeral of a family friend in a barn in Ohio. I was in eleven prisons in five days in upstate New York, and then at the Fall Revival Meetings at Bowmansville Mennonite in Lancaster County, PA. I helped at a neighbor's household auction in Benton and sang at a family Christmas banquet, in October, in New Holland, PA. I sang in a friend's basement for eighteen people; at the Holmes County Flea Market with people milling around; and at the Encounter in New York with 2,500 folks in attendance. The month ended with world champion female basketball handler, Tanya Crevier, doing two days of clinics.

There were high school chapels and assemblies and speaking at our CGM Annual Fall Banquet before we ended up at Mercer prison in Pennsylvania on Halloween night (with a full moon). I was gone thirteen days in October. The plans for Lydia and the children to meet me in Lancaster in the middle of this tour and then fly home with Bruce Hummel fell through when one by one, each of the children had better offers come along in the way of school activities. At least eighty-two decisions were made in the New York and Pennsylvania prisons, and several decisions for recommitment were made at Bowmansville. I am writing this (finally) on November 1 in a state of rest and relaxation. Whew!

THANKSGIVING

We, of all people, have so much to be thankful for. I try to be thankful every day, but ever since September 11, I have been even more thankful for every day, realizing that things can happen fast, and being reminded that I have no guarantee of tomorrow (or my next heartbeat). Each day is a gift of God and I want to live it abundantly (John 10:10). On top of being thankful for the gift of life and the family and health and ministry that God has given me, the ministry of Common Ground also has much to be thankful for:

- The Office Complex of the International Headquarters of Common Ground Ministries (the barn) is 98 percent complete; in other words, as complete as it's going to be for a year or so. We moved in during the summer, and for the first time, it is a joy to be in the office and do the necessary paper shuffling and planning that a small ministry requires. It's still not my favorite chore, but a pleasant office makes it so much easier. (And it's close.)

- The Bus. We're going to get a bus! Last winter a businessman from Greenwood, DE, said if we would raise $50,000, he would give the rest to help us buy a touring bus! We had been thinking of upgrading our motorhome, but this was beyond our wildest dreams! Not much has been said in the newsletter because I wanted to be sure that we had the man's permission to rejoice publicly. There will be more information coming, but it looks like the bus might be ready in November!

HAPPY THANKSGIVING!!

November - 2001

THE LEPER

"Nobody has touched me for five years... I have not touched another human being for five years not my wife; not my daughter; I have not even felt a slap on my back from my brother after one of his funny stories... five years...!"

These were some of the laments of a good friend of mine in prison who has the most dreaded of all diseases; leprosy!

Actually, his name is John Lemasters, from Virginia, and he portrayed "The Leper" in a one-man drama in six Ohio prisons last month. The parallels between a leper and a prisoner are many: they are isolated, outcasts, untouchable, separated from their families... and John's dramatic presentation seemed to touch a nerve in every prison we visited. I am used to seeing men respond in a prison chapel service, but the response to "The Leper" was different in that the men couldn't wait for the invitation! Over sixty men came forward in six prisons to be touched by Jesus! He still touches those who come to Him.

MERRY CHRISTMAS!

Tonight (November 29) I begin the "banquet trail." I will be singing at a company Christmas banquet, even though it is still November and there is no snow. In our community, there are so many companies who treat their employees to a banquet at this time of the year and I get the privilege of being involved by being the entertainment. Some singers don't like being labeled as entertainers, but my outlook on that is that if a singer is not very entertaining, no one will listen to him. But if I'm only entertainment, although they might listen, I will not have said anything of eternal value.

entertain v. 1. to hold the attention of; 2. to extend hospitality towards; 3. to hold in mind; 4. to continue with; MAINTAIN

So, my goal is to tell the story of Jesus in an entertaining way, mixed in with interesting stories—songs—so that it is received gladly. Or, maybe it's the other way around; sing interesting and sometimes funny stories—songs—to gain the attention and acceptance of the audience, and then tell—sing—

the old, old story. However you look at it, I love this time of the year. For an hour or so I am an insider in the company and I enjoy the food and fellowship of so many friends. It's the easiest time of the year to talk about the One who came as a baby in a manger, grew into a man in the grace and knowledge of God, died on a cross for our sins and rose from the dead that we might all have eternal life.

No wonder we sing, *Joy To The World! Let earth receive her King!* May your heart prepare Him room and may you have a blessed Christmas this year.

Joy to the World!

December - 2001

2002!

What a year 2001 was! Everything that happened during the last year is overshadowed by the tragic events of September 11. We will never forget the horror and disbelief of what we saw and heard on that fateful day. Our lives will never be the same.

And yet in my personal life and in the life of my family and in Common Ground Ministries, it was a wonderful year. I personally grew in wisdom and in knowledge of the Lord Jesus Christ through study, reading, prayer, ministry, and fellowship with other believers. (I also grew physically, which was not one of my goals, but it is symbolic of God's abundant provision). The letters I get from prisoners tell me that our ministry has made a difference in many lives. And when a prisoner is changed by Jesus Christ, that means that there are potentially many others who will not be robbed, abused, abandoned, etc., but may actually be helped by a now productive citizen.

The family seems to be doing well. Adam got his driver's license in January of 2001 and drove a whole year with no accidents, citations, or even any close calls (as far as we know). We went deer hunting last month and Adam got a ten-point buck on the first day of gun season! (This is a one-page newsletter, so there's not enough space to tell you the whole deer story). Amy and Katie played volleyball on their respective teams at Central Christian School and Katie is also playing basketball. Lydia completed her first whole year as secretary for CGM and is doing very well.

In November we took possession of a 1984 MCI 40' motor coach with a new conversion due to the generosity of Sam Yoder of Delaware, and many of you. On our first trip the engine lost all its oil, which means we lost the engine, and again, Sam Yoder helped us, so we are on the road again. We did not lose the oil plug as first thought, but the result was the same; a nut came off the alternator and its gear went into the engine and tore things up.

I took part in seventy prison services, forty-some church services, a camp, a mission trip, several Wingfield Encounters, twenty-one(!) banquets in December, 114 days away from home, and a total of 220 services in twenty different states proclaiming Christ in the year of 2001.

Time is one thing that we all have the same amount of. I have just as much as George Bush does. What I do with it is not unimportant. It is not a renewable resource. Once it's gone, it's gone. And one day, it's going to run out. The Bible implies that the time is coming when "time will be no more." That's why Paul says to be careful how you live, not as fools, but as wise, redeeming the time. Pray with me that I (and you) will redeem the time—make the most of every opportunity—all year long in 2002.

January - 2002

OUT OF AFRICA

"You need to come to Africa. My people would like your singing." These were the first words that Bishop Henry Mulandi spoke to me when I first met him at a friend's house twelve years ago. Although I used to fear that God would call me to Africa, now I had a desire to go, but it didn't seem to fit into the goals of our ministry. But after being invited every year for twelve years, it finally seemed right, and I went with a work/evangelistic team headed by pastor Dennis Mullet.

What a place! Africa is huge, wild, kind, harsh, awesome. During the day, our team of twelve *mzungus* (white people) helped in the construction of a church in Thika, Kenya, a small town about forty-five minutes northwest of Nairobi. In the evenings we held evangelistic campaigns in two nearby villages. Bishop Mulandi was our host. He has been to my house here in Benton, and now my daughter Amy and I had the privilege to be guests in his home for a week.

The church will seat 4,000 when finished, so as you can imagine, we didn't make much of a dent in the construction, but every little bit helps. In the evening services, we saw people come to the Lord each night. In the village of Gatuikira, thirty-some people made first-time commitments during the week. A similar number came to faith in the village of Kabati. Each night Amy and I sang, and then I would preach. Although English is the official language in Kenya, Swahili is the language of the people, so everything was done through interpretation. Even when I was finished preaching, the local pastors would close the meetings in Swahili interpreted into Kikuyo, the local tribal language.

We ended the trip with a safari. I was amazed to see zebras, elephants, hippos, rhinos, lions—all the animals I've always heard of when Africa is mentioned—just wandering around in their natural habitat! No fences; although it was a game reserve, it was not a zoo. We stayed in our vehicles or risked being lunch.

The highlight of the whole trip for me was the privilege we had to hold a Maasai church service for the staff of the safari lodge. The Maasai are the most traditional, the most feared, the fiercest of the forty-two tribes of Kenya. There are very few Christians among them. This is the group that drinks milk mixed with blood from their cows. The man at the entrance gate saw the words "church bus" on our vehicle and asked if we would preach for the staff. I've been to hundreds of hotels in my day, and this was the first time I was ever asked to preach to the staff. Usually, they tell me to be quiet.

After supper, we went to a small building several hundred

yards down the path and heard the quiet singing of twenty-eight Maasai Christians. Our group sang and I preached from John 2. They were so thankful. They wondered if we couldn't stay for several days and hold meetings. We promised to send them some study Bibles and pray about coming back. In all, we worked six days. I sang and preached nine times. Now I understand why people are drawn to Africa. What a place!

February - 2002

LESSONS FROM PINECRAFT

When people ask me how I learned to play guitar, I'm always tempted to answer that I'm still learning (which is true). When I had been playing for about a year, I went to Florida (1972) with some friends and stayed in greater downtown Pinecraft. Almost every night I found myself in someone's living room or back porch, playing the fifteen songs I knew over and over. For six weeks I played every night to crowds of at least ten, sometimes up to fifteen people. About the third week, I began to notice something—my guitar playing was coming to me so naturally that I wasn't even thinking about it. I was able to develop some new licks, which now come to me almost subconsciously. Playing every night was the best practice there was. So, how did I learn to play guitar? I went to Pinecraft!

Well, I just got back yesterday from Pinecraft. I was there to be a part of the Gospel Express Benefit Auction. That is always a great time for me, to be a part of such a worthy cause and see so many friends (and miss a couple days of snow). But this time I had memories of thirty years ago. I sang fourteen times in the six days I was there! The crowd sizes ranged from ten or twelve people in a house to close to 1,000 at the tent. I sang at three churches, two restaurants, three trailer parks, several living rooms, and four times at the auction tent. And to really bring back memories, I saw several friends from Pennsylvania who were with me in 1972! Theirs was one of the living room concerts. The only problem was, they requested songs that I haven't sung for twenty years. What a blast!

So what? That is always the bottom line question I ask myself after singing or speaking, especially if it was in a non-church setting. Did my presence make any eternal difference, or did I just have a good time? After singing Tuesday night at the 50's Diner parking lot, next to Der Dutchman, a man came to me with tears in his eyes. He said, "Keep singing that song, 'Reachable' (by Steve Chapman). My son ran off to Florida when he was young, and we kept praying and after several years he came back and now he is a preacher." This man was touched by a song and he encouraged me to keep on encouraging others through song. There were similar stories each time I sang. So, I've decided to keep on singing.

Other lessons? I was reminded of how I got proficient on the guitar. I play a very simple style, but there are several lessons in my Pinecraft guitar story:

- If you do something enough times, you might get good at it. Practice.

- One of the best ways to learn to do something is to do it! Just do it!

- "All hard work brings a profit..." (Proverbs 14:23 NIV)

"your labor in the Lord is not in vain" (I Corinthians 15:58). Work!

• When you find your niche in life, God can use you even when you're doing what you love to do, and life becomes an exciting adventure. (Who said this? (besides my Dad) "If you love your job, you'll never have to work a day in your life!") Find your niche.

Maybe King David in Psalm 37 could sum this up best: "Delight thyself in the Lord and He shall give thee the desires of thine heart."

March - 2002

THE RAMIFICATIONS OF AN ACT OF KINDNESS

Many times in a prison chapel I wonder how many lives have been affected negatively by the crime of just one of these men. The ripples of sin go on for miles and years. On the other hand, I just received a story from an old (longtime) friend, retired LAM missionary Bill Brown, who tells how one act of kindness is still reaping benefits thirty-three years later.

Bill went back to Costa Rica last July for a national church meeting. The president of the Costa Rican Bible Churches, Luis Rodriquez, was driving Bill to one of the meetings when Bill asked him how he had come to know the Lord. "A relative named Felipe Beirute led me to the Lord," he said. Felipe! Bill then told this story:

It was 1969 and we were to move out of our rented house. A couple rang our doorbell and told us that they were to move into the house that day. We said we had rented the house until the end of the month. They showed us a receipt giving them rights to the house on the 15th; we showed them our receipt giving us rights until the 30th.

They explained that they were looking in the newspaper for a house to rent. They dialed the wrong number and got the owner of our house. He said he hadn't put an ad in the paper but he had a house to rent, so they rented it. Now they had no place to go and we didn't either. What should we do?

We decided to share the house with them for the remainder of the two weeks. We were a family of five and they of nine! The house was small. In the evenings we would sit around the table and talk. The conversation turned to the things of God, often continuing until the wee hours of the morning. One night don Felipe and his wife, Yolanda, trusted Christ. They lived fruitful lives until their deaths, and all seven of their children came to know and serve the Lord... and a young relative, Luis Rodriquez, as well.

From one dialing error, a family of nine trusted Christ. Felipe was a lay pastor for a number of years and he lead Luis Rodriquez to Christ, who in turn won his family, and who became a longtime pastor and president of our church association. And who knows where it will end?

When that doorbell rang, we didn't have the foggiest

idea that God was presenting us with a marvelous opportunity to witness. In fact, it was very inconvenient. But the Lord moved us to open our house to them. I don't like to think what we (and they) would have missed out on if we had turned them away.

This sounds just like the Bill and Lori Brown that we knew in Costa Rica. He is always ready in season and out of season. I wonder how many opportunities I have squandered because it wasn't convenient. The next time someone knocks on my door, I hope God brings this story to my mind. The ripples of a kind act can go on for miles and years.

April - 2002

A PRISONER RESPONDS
(TO LAST MONTH'S NEWSLETTER)

I read your "Ramifications of an Act of Kindness." In all these years of being in prison I hardly knew nor found a true act of kindness. From the age of 16 to 44, my life was drugs and alcohol. When I was around 8 years old I accepted Christ as my Savior, even many times dedicated my life to becoming a minister, but I just could not find forgiveness for my actions. Even more, I could not forgive myself.

Two years ago I found myself in the hole [solitary confinement] for the 4th time. On the 63rd day of being in the hole, I got down on my hands and knees. As always, I did not find the forgiveness that I felt I did not deserve. But I did tell God I had no control anymore, that I was overweight, a piece of junk and a real slob. I didn't make any promises because I had broken every promise I had ever made to God. If He would only take away my addiction, I would at least try.

Well, after two years of walking the track, lifting weights and mowing the prison lawn with a non-powered lawn mower, reading my Bible and praying every day, I can hold my head up again. The true act of kindness for me was God & Christ coming into my life. I could not live without Him today...

-ERNEST, MISSOURI

Ernest went on to say that his life is in order now and things are going well, even though he is in prison. I wonder how much sooner his life would have straightened out if someone had shown him an "act of kindness" when he was younger?

BUSY MONTH

April started out with our fall banquet in Hartville and will end up visiting the Gospel Echoes Banquet in Walnut Creek. I had eight prison services and two prison ministry benefit auctions; one with the Echoes in Indiana and the other with the Gospel Express in Pennsylvania. I also sang at a benefit concert in Pennsylvania for The Lighthouse (industry for the handicapped) and Welsh Mountain Home. I had the privilege of being a part of a Bill Glass Day of Champions in Tulsa, OK. On Saturday, April 20, I was in four prison services in Tulsa with Rich Garza, former NFL football player for the Cincinnati Bengals. With four different speakers and singers, there were over 300 decisions in Tulsa Prison that day! While in Oklahoma I preached at Zion Mennonite Church in Pryor and had a concert there that evening. This weekend I was asked to fill in for seminar speaker Alva Mast who was called out of town for a funeral. I had to hurry home from New Holland, PA, to be with Light in the Valley Chapel. It turned out to be a blessing!

May - 2002

GOD IS GOOD

If I say that theological truth—God is good—in a prison chapel, the response is always instant and loud: "ALL THE TIME!" Then if I say, "All the time," the response is an even louder, "GOD IS GOOD!" The truth is, God is good all the time. Sometimes we get so caught up in our little worlds that we fail to realize, at least here in America, how blessed we are and how good God is. If I were to say "God is good" in our churches, the response would be a few blank stares and several nods. Why is it that we have to be down and out or persecuted before we realize how nice we had it and how good our God really is?

One of the by-products of going into prisons and taking mission trips overseas is that I see how nice we have it here and how blessed I am. I wonder if I could say, "God is good" if I lived in Kenya, where Amy and I were this January; or in Latin America, where we lived for seven years as missionaries, not as local citizens; or in India; or China... Could I praise God from a prison cell like men do every time I visit their prison? One thing is for sure—no matter how bad things may get for me or my family, I know this: God is good. All the time.

I just re-read this. Things are not bad for us. We are doing great, much better than we deserve. God is good!

SUMMER TRIP (GO WEST, YOUNG MAN)

Our June tour schedule is coming together. We will be in the Federal Correctional Institute in Tucson, AZ, for several services on June 8 and 9, and then after a church service in Tucson or Phoenix. After that, we will head for the Montana State Prison for several chapel services, and then to a church in Deer Lodge. Then we are scheduled to be at Bonner's Ferry, ID, for several days.

As you know, we don't really have to go that far to find needs in prisons, but this will be a test for the new bus that was provided for our ministry. It will probably be our last opportunity to travel as a family for a while. Next year Adam will be a senior, Amy a sophomore, and Katie will be in eighth grade. I can't believe it, but they are beginning to make plans of their own! It's been great being able to do some programs and services as a family over the years, and we are looking forward to this (final?) family tour.

As you read this, we should be in Arizona. Thank you for your faithful support. Have a great summer! God Bless you!

June - 2002

HOW AWESOME IS THIS PLACE!

These words of Jacob came to my mind as I gazed out at the Grand Canyon. When Jacob made that statement in Genesis, he was awed by the presence of God. When I looked out on the Grand Canyon, I didn't see angels ascending and descending like Jacob did, but I, too, was awed by the presence of God. His handiwork was so amazing that all I could do was stare. "The Heavens declare the glory of God; and the firmament (i.e. Grand Canyon) sheweth His handiwork" (Psalm 19:1).

Amy and I had a similar experience in January of this year when we were heading North out of Nairobi, Kenya, in Africa and all of a sudden, the earth just seemed to drop down for a mile on the left side of the highway. The view was breathtaking. We could see for miles! We learned that we were seeing the Great Rift Valley, a giant rift in the earth that runs from Kenya up into Egypt. At the time, I had never seen the Grand Canyon, but I didn't think it could be more amazing than this. Well, I've come to the conclusion that one amazing work of God on this planet is just as awesome as another! *How awesome is this place!*

TUCSON FEDERAL PRISON

Another awesome place was the chapel at the Tucson Federal Prison, and this time it was definitely not because of the scenery, but because of God's presence (the chapel was sort of ugly and sterile). After separate men and women's services on Saturday, I came back on Sunday for a Spanish service. Even though my Spanish was accented and rusty, God used the songs and the sermon to touch the hearts of the sixty men who came out to see what this gringo had to say. In fact, one man even said, *"Toco mi corazon!"* (He touched my heart!) Twelve of these men made new commitments to Christ. I could say with Jacob, "Surely the Lord is in this place!"

We also had four services at the Montana State Prison in Deer Lodge, MT, as well as the Alcohol Treatment Center and the Juvenile Boot Camp.

THE MOST BEAUTIFUL SIGHT IN AMERICA

We live in the greatest country in the world. If you doubt that, I challenge you to go anywhere else in the world. Nowhere else could I travel 6,000 miles and use the same language, the same currency, fuel up without cash, stay at modern camp-grounds, see awesome scenery and wonders of nature... add to that the fact that in this culture I am not even close to being considered rich. To quote Russian comedian Yakov Smirnoff; "What a country!" But after seeing the Grand Canyon, Glacier National Park, the beautiful desert hills of New Mexico, the Great Salt Lake, the farmland from Idaho to Ohio... the most beautiful sight of our longest tour in several years was in Benton, OH, when we saw our front yard! There's no place like home. How awesome is this place!

July - 2002

WHAT A TIME THAT WILL BE!

One of the wonderful promises of the gospel is that one day we will all be together with God the Father in a place called Heaven. The Bible attempts to describe that place to us, but it is just too awesome for our finite minds to comprehend. Paul simply quotes one of the prophets: "No eye has seen, no ear has heard, and no mind has imagined what God has prepared for those who love him" (1 Corinthians 2:9).

Jesus tried to bring it down to our level when He described Heaven like this: "The kingdom of God is like... a sower; a mustard seed; yeast; a hidden treasure; a pearl; a fishnet..." When He was finished with all these parables in Matthew 13, He asked, "Have you understood all these things?" and they replied, "Yes." But I wonder if they really did.

I have been thinking of Heaven lately, probably because of my age, the loss of a close friend, the condition of the world, and my high school reunion! Yes, I think I got a taste of what one aspect of Heaven may be like at my thirty-fifth class reunion. I went around shaking hands with old classmates (old means former, but in this case it also means old), laughing at old stories, trying to guess names without looking at the name tag, and just hanging out with friends, some of whom I have known since I was one year old. It was a two-night affair, with Friday being a fancy dinner and Saturday a come-as-you-are pizza supper. What a time of reminiscing, reconnecting, and just enjoying old friends.

I left the reunion at 10:00 pm on Saturday and drove until 2:30 am to Michigan for a Sunday noon concert at a folk festival. I had plenty of time to ruminate and think about all my friends and how their lives have turned out and what will happen to them when their time on earth is done. Some have been very successful. Some aren't doing very well. Some have had tragedy in their lives and others seem to sail through life with no problems.

I think what our parents told us since we were young is finally sinking into some of our fifty-three-year-old brains: life isn't fair. But life is eternal. We will live forever; either in a place of indescribable peace and joy called Heaven or in a place of indescribable horror called Hell. What makes the difference? Well, again, there's an old saying, "It's who you know." If you know Jesus, you're in. If not, you're at the wrong reunion. It sounds too simple, and there is a little more to it than that, but the basic truth is, "...no one comes to [Heaven] except through [Jesus]."

Get to know Him. I want to see you at that Reunion. I can't force you to come. I was on the school reunion committee and we sent letters and made phone calls and we did all we could, but some just didn't want to come. I think it was their loss. We had a great time. I am also on the Heaven reunion committee (as are all Christians). Here is your letter. Come! The directions are in a book called the Bible. Committee members are plentiful. Ask for directions! But be there! What a time that will be!

August - 2002

SUMMER, 2002!

Summer is over! Can you believe it? The children are back in school and I am back in prison. But what a great, wonderful, fast summer we had!

August is over! I am writing this on the 30th, which is a little late for the newsletter deadline, but this month, have I got an excuse for you! My vehicle was broken into on August 3 and my laptop computer and my briefcase were stolen. I had to drive eight hours to Little Eden camp with the wind whistling in my left ear. I was the speaker for the week, while some thief was walking around with my Bible, my Daytimer, my sermon notes, my glasses, the tape player, my... well, every day I think of something else that's missing. And all the while, he was writing bad checks in my name. Although insurance covers the monetary value, some things are irreplaceable.

There was a time when this would have bothered me, but last May, when my friend Joe Miller Jr. died, I was reminded that there are only a few things in life that are really important, and getting a few things stolen is not one of them. Yes, it's irritating and unhandy, and I feel violated and all that stuff, but ruin my day? No way. I am praying, however, that my Bible and other things will be returned, and that someday I will have the opportunity to sing about the love of Jesus to this man in a Spirit-filled prison chapel.

From Little Eden, we (Lydia, Katie, and I) went directly to Philadelphia, PA, to be one the three singing groups that sang all day long on the sidewalk at the Reading Terminal Market. The weekend also included attending an Amish church service and a concert at a riding arena. We then sang at the Holmes County Fair, a trail ride at Salt Fork, a retreat in South Carolina, and at six prison services with Steve Wingfield at Lewisburg, PA. Tonight I sing on the Square of Berlin and Sunday at the Walnut Creek Mennonite Church picnic. On Labor Day, summer is unofficially over! Time flies!

September - 2002

LONDON PRISON FREEDOM RALLY A SUCCESS!

This was just one of the comments heard at the London Correctional Facility during the Freedom Rally held September 20-22, 2002:

> I have been incarcerated for twenty-two years straight, starting at the age of eighteen. I have never seen anything like this in any of the five institutions I have been to. The kindness and love that was present and prevalent at this rally showed me that there is still love in the world. Maybe I can forgive myself for the crime I committed.
>
> -INMATE AT LONDON CORRECTIONAL

For about ten years I have been working with the Gospel Echoes to try to bring a Freedom Rally to an Ohio institution. They do them in other states and they were ready and willing to come here, but the Ohio system was very hesitant. Several years ago we began presenting the idea to Chaplains Cahill and Davis at the London Correctional Facility because they were very open to the idea. Glendon Bender came out to London several times over the past two years to present the program, the chaplains would present it to the warden, and the central office would reject it. But finally this year it got a reluctant approval ("We've never done it this way before...") so we began making plans. Then it was called off. Then it was back on, but no barbecue. Then, within a month of the scheduled rally, the institution changed wardens!

To make a long story short, the new warden got behind the idea that was thrust upon him. He paved the way for us to provide a meal for the 2,400 inmates on Friday night and have meetings and concerts all day Saturday and a worship service on Sunday morning. Two hundred and twenty-two (222!) volunteers signed up to help cook, feed, counsel, and be in the prison for the weekend!

Many inmates told me that they had never seen such an atmosphere in the prison or in the mess hall. "The mess hall is a place to go eat and get out. Don't talk to anyone. But Friday night there was actually fellowship going on! And the food was delicious! That's the first Pepsi I've had in twelve years."

The meal consisted of hamburgers and hot dogs that were barbecued just outside the fence, potato salad from Der Dutchmen Restaurant, and a Pepsi. As the men headed for their seats, a volunteer handed each one a Bible. The chaplain said that outsiders feeding the whole prison has never happened in Ohio before. As we sang and preached on the platform out in the prison yard, up to several hundred prisoners gathered around to listen while the rest of the prison played football, lifted weights, jogged, and basically went about their daily prison routine. But the chaplain said, "Don't let that fool you. They're listening."

We haven't tallied up the number of responses yet, but the accounts we have will never tell the whole story. Praise the Lord for the commitments, but pray for those hardened, bitter, cynical men who—for the first time in a long time—were shown that someone cares. Some were moved just one step closer to God's love. They're still lost, but they have seen a gleam of light at the edge of the woods. Maybe they will start walking toward the light, out of the woods. In fact, one old inmate came up to me with a smile on his face and a tattoo of a spider on his bald head and said, "I don't believe in all this stuff, but I've never seen anything like this in my eighteen years of prison life." Thank you, volunteers and those who contributed financially for the food and Bibles.

October - 2002

THANKSGIVING

When we lived overseas I was always aware of how thankful I should be when I compared my situation to that of the average person in Latin America. Now that I am involved in prison ministry, I am again made aware of how blessed I am to have been brought up in a stable, happy home with two parents who were committed to each other and to us children (and still are, after fifty-seven years). I was born in a country of opportunity, and into a community with a godly heritage and ethic.

Last week after a chapel service, a prisoner named David told me this heartbreaking story (with a happy ending?) that demonstrates the results of bad choices and sinful practices and how God can make something beautiful out of the tangled messes we get ourselves into:

This is my third number (number = prison sentence). I was arrested for the first time twenty-two years ago. My daughter was born that very day. I went off to prison and never got to see her. When I got out, my wife had left and I don't know where she is. I've still never seen my daughter, but I pray for her every day. I got this "number" two years ago here in Ohio. About two months ago I got a letter from my daughter! She was passing through this city and stopped in at the courthouse to see if she could find my name, and since I had been through the court system here, she found me! She's been searching for me for several years! We've written several letters back and forth and when I get out in two weeks, she is going to pick me up!

Think of it! The first time this man is going to meet his twenty-two-year-old daughter is when she picks him up from prison! He never held her as a baby. He missed her first steps. He never heard her say, "Daddy!" Wasted years. What a promise we have in Joel 2:25, 26: "I will restore to you the years that the locusts have eaten ... praise the name of the Lord your God, that hath dealt wondrously with you: and my people shall never be ashamed."

It makes me even more thankful for good parents and now a good wife and happy children.

Larry Skrant, the speaker at our Fall Banquet, tells of the letter he got from his eight-year-old daughter when he was in prison:

Dear Daddy,

My name is Stephanie. Do you remember me?

That simple childlike question broke his heart, and it was a step in bringing him to his senses. He eventually became a Christian. He is now out of prison, working at a good job, beginning a prison ministry, being a father to his daughters, and speaking at prison banquets.

What a mighty God we serve! May we never forget His blessings! May this Thanksgiving be a time of remembering His mighty works. His blessings. His provision. May you and your family be blessed.

HAPPY THANKSGIVING!

November - 2002

FEDERAL CORRECTIONAL

There is one federal prison in Ohio, located in Elkton (near Youngstown). It is about five years old, and we had never been there. Several months ago I made contact with the chaplain and introduced our ministry. I told him what we do and that we would be glad to offer our services to his chapel program. He said that they were well taken care of with outside groups, but thanks for calling. I said, "Praise the Lord! If there are that many people going into prisons, our country may be headed in the right direction!"

After a pause, he said what they really needed was someone to do services in Spanish. I didn't say anything. Then he asked if I speak Spanish. I always hesitate when asked that question, because it's been fourteen years since I lived in Costa Rica, but I said, "Yes."

"You do?" he asked.

"Yes," I said.

"Well, when can you come?"

That began the process. I contacted fellow Spanish speaker Randy Keim and we went into the "big house" on November 15.

There were about sixty-five Latinos from at least ten different countries at the service. I sang, Randy preached, and then I sang again. It was a lively service, just like a typical Costa Rican worship service. In the confusion of languages, no invitation to follow Christ was given, but we got an open door for an ongoing ministry and an invitation to come back. Gracias a Dios!

December - 2002

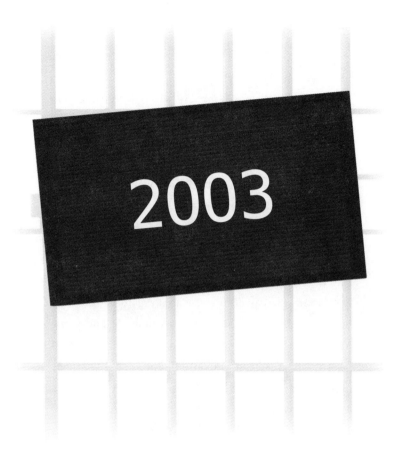

2003

HAPPY NEW YEAR!

Someone once asked for a statement that would always be current, no matter what the circumstances. The reply he got was, "And it came to pass." Yes, here we are in the year of our Lord 2003 and it has passed again. It seems like the Lord gives us so many chances to start afresh; each 24-hour period His mercies are new; every seven days we start a new week; every thirty days, a new month; and now we start a new year. Allow me to quote a good friend and mentor, Dr. Dennis Kinlaw, from his new devotional:

This Day With The Master:

January 1

The new year brings hope. As we look into the year that opens before us, we would like to think that it could be better than the one behind us. That yearning for something better is a gift from God and a promise that the hope can be realized. God wants the year before you to be the best that you have ever had...

If you are yearning for a better year, you are exercising your God-given gift to want the best. And just like a good parent, God wants your year to be better even more than you do! I am looking forward to the best year I have ever had. I have even made some New Year's resolutions (goals). My prayer is that you will have the best year of your life in 2003. Last year was great for me. It wasn't easy. I lost some good friends to death. I was away from home more than I like to be. There were some hills to climb (at least they weren't mountains). But there were victories won. Some prisoners were set free. Some church members were awakened. God's word went forth and will not return void. It was a great year! May you enter 2003 with confidence. May this be your greatest year of life! The best is yet to be!

January - 2003

THE POWER OF A WORD, OF A LIFE

Twenty-three of us left for Costa Rica on the 17th of January for two weeks of work, ministry, fellowship, beach, and changed lives. Reuben and Linda Beachy asked me to help them lead their Gospel Haven youth group on a mission trip. They could have done it themselves, but they wanted me to go along and I didn't think I should argue. This trip was a highlight of the twenty-some short-term mission trips I have been with. Here's why:

In 1992, I was planning to go a small village in Northern Costa Rica to help build a church. Mark Coblentz told fellow church member, truck driver Harold Troyer, "You should go." Harold replied, "I might go, but I ain't getting up in church and speaking like they do when they get back." Well, Harold lied. He went along and when he got back, he spoke in churches!He was so changed by the trip that the next year he went with me again, and then the next year he and Debbie led a team themselves. They have been doing so every year since.

Three years ago, two of the local young folks who went with Harold were so touched by the experience that they signed up to be three-year missionaries with Christ For the Cities Missions. This year, on my 21st team, our leaders on the field were Angie Raber and Andy Yoder, Spanish-speaking Dutchmen who came with Harold three years ago and will also lead Harold's team this month!

UPDATE: Andy is now a medical doctor in Columbus, Ohio. From an 8th grade education (Amish don't attend High School) to M.D.!

Paul wrote to Timothy; "And the things you have heard me say in the presence of many witnesses entrust to reliable people who will also be qualified to teach others" (2 Timothy 2:2 NIV). It was so good to see the full circle—I took Harold, he took Andy and Angie, and now they are leading many Costa Ricans and us!

What if Harold had not gone in 1992? Well, for one thing, no one would have noticed anything strange or out of the ordinary. Harold's business would have continued to grow, he would still be a faithful church attendee, over 100 short-term missionaries would have never gone to Central America, and ten church buildings that are currently housing congregations would not exist in Costa Rica. Andy and Angie and several other Holmes County ministers would still be working and living in Holmes County and by all outside appearances would be doing well, and hundreds of Costa Rican Christians would still be living in darkness...

I could go on, but I'm trying to tell you that one obedient life can make a big difference. And you don't have to be a brain surgeon for this to happen. Harold is an ordinary man, eighth-grade education, can't sing or dance (well, maybe a little), and he is not a great orator. He just does what he can and it is significant. I'm reminded of the old movie, *It's A Wonderful Life*, where George Bailey finds out how different the world would be if he had never been born.

And not only can one obedient life make a huge eternal difference; sometimes a word changes everything. What if Mark Coblentz had not encouraged Harold to go? From what I understand, Mark said one sentence: "Harold, you should go."

No wonder the Bible has so much to say about our speech. Solomon said in Proverbs 15:23, "A word spoken in due season, how good it is!" And, in 25:11, "A word fitly spoken is like apples of gold in pictures of silver."

A word is powerful! Your life lived in obedience to Christ is powerful! You can make a difference! I did. Mark did. Harold did. If we can, anybody can! Be obedient! Follow Christ.

February - 2003

THE LION AND THE LAMB

"March comes in like a lion and goes out like a lamb." Have you ever heard that old saying? It looks like the first half of that proverb is going to be true this year as winter hangs on longer than it has for the last few years. We came back from Florida and Nashville on the last day of February, so as I write this (late again), March is roaring in with snow and cold. The biggest blizzards in history have been in March. Hopefully, it will go out like a lamb; warm and spring-like.

As I look at the events in the world right now, I am reminded of another analogy of a Lion and a Lamb. Two thousand years ago, God came into our world as a Lamb. He was born in a barn; He was meek and lowly. He was led to slaughter; as a sheep before its shearers is silent, so He opened not his mouth. He was crucified (executed), buried, and rose from the dead and He now sits at the right hand of the Father in heaven. The Bible informs us that someday He will come back, and when He does, it won't be as a lamb; it will be more like a lion.

"Then I saw heaven opened, and behold, a white horse! The One sitting on it is called Faithful and True, and in righteousness he judges and makes war...

And the armies in heaven, arrayed in fine linen, white and pure, were following him on white horses. From his mouth comes a sharp sword with which to strike down the nations, and he will rule them with a rod of iron. He will tread the winepress of the fury of the wrath of God the Almighty" (Revelation 19:11, 14, 15 ESV).

He came in like a Lamb and will come back like a Lion. We've had two thousand years to prepare. Are you ready?

The underlying purpose of our ministry is to help and even warn people to be ready. The first time He came, He was persuasive and patient. When He comes again there will be no time to go get oil for your lamp. His patience is wearing thin and when He comes again it will be to gather His own. I think one reason the Bible calls it *that great and terrible day* is because for those who are ready, it will be great, and for those who are not ready, it will terrible. The horror of what could happen in our current world situation cannot even compare to the horror of not being ready when the Lion comes. I urge you—get ready. Turn to Jesus, our only hope. You don't have to fear the Lion. He wants to be your Savior. When? Today is the day of salvation. In all of world history, only two days really matter: "This" day and "That" day! Prepare for "That" day today!

March - 2003

HOWARD GRAY

I have been singing the song "Howard Gray" for a little over ten years after I first heard it sung by Gary Hall. I called Lee Domann, who wrote the song, and got permission to record it in 1989. I have sung the song a thousand times since then, always with some kind of emotional response from the audience, whether it be prisoners, school children, or concert goers. Last month, when I sang at the National Frame Builders Association at the Opryland Hotel, I called Lee Domann, who lives in Nashville, and asked if he would come to my concert and sing his song. He very graciously agreed. In the course of the concert, I sang the song first and then introduced Lee as the man who wrote about this true story. He then sang it and told the rest of the story.

Lee sang this song as contractors and business owners listened, and then he told the story of how he met Howard Gray twenty some years after this incident. Lee's dad had died back in Kansas and Howard came to the funeral. Lee was able to ask for forgiveness after all those years.

I meet Howard Grays in every prison I visit, in every school, workplace... even at the coffee shop. I have been Howard Gray, and I have been Lee Domann. Of the many lessons in this story, I will mention this one: Messing up (sinning) is part of the human experience, but there is a Biblical way to go about making it right, and the sooner the better. Don't wait twenty years.

April - 2003

GOOD REPORT ON
COSTA RICA WORK TEAM

I just received a letter from Andy Yoder, missionary in Costa Rica. The church that our January work team helped to build in Upala was not finished when we left, but the local folks said they would not stop working until it was completed. We left with the rafters up and the roof purlins on. Andy writes:

> Hey, my friend, how are things up North? I just wanted to tell you that Pastor Daniel called from Upala yesterday and he gave me an update on how things are going at the church since the gringos left in January. First, he tells me that he got the stuff you sent him and he says Muchas Gracias. They just had an open house for the church the other day and what a turn-out they had! They had around five hundred people show up from the village and other churches. Five pastors from five different churches came as well. The church is now finished and is being used. Daniel told me that when he talks with the people from the village about the work team they still, to this day, start crying. It sounds like the team really left a lasting impact on the community. It was also a great encouragement for me to hear this as I trust it is for you, knowing that the work you are doing is touching and changing lives not only back home, but here as well.
>
> God bless,
> Andy

Well, let me tell you, I can go a lot of miles on a letter like that. What an encouragement! I keep harping on the fact that in prison ministry as well as short-term mission trips, ninety percent of ministry is simply showing up. Your presence is much more valuable than your presents. And I'm not even counting what that trip did to change our hearts! You just can't out-give God, not financially, time-wise, with service, or otherwise. We always receive more than we give. "As cold waters to a thirsty soul, so is good news from a far country" (Proverbs 25:25).

EL SALVADOR

Since this letter is so late, it gives me the opportunity to report on my wife Lydia and our daughter Amy's trip to El Salvador. Ten folks from our church (MCA) teamed up with eight people from Berlin Christian Fellowship (BCF) and went to Santa Ana, El Salvador, in Central America. They spent a week doing construction and also working with children and ladies in a very poor section of town. They came home last night and were glowing in the glory of God. In the heat and poverty of that country, God used these gringos to touch hearts and used those poor people to touch the gringo's hearts. They showed up and ministry happened.

May - 2003

HARVEST TIME

Lord willing, by the time you read this, Adam and I will be in a Texas wheat field, driving a combine or a truck, working on the wheat harvest! I will have spoken at two high school graduations (Faith Christian Academy in Wilmot and Central Christian in Kidron, where Adam graduated) and six prisons. I will have had three concerts, a dozen graduation parties (including one for Adam here at home), numerous other meetings to get ready for a Wingfield Encounter here in July, and will have packed for our six-week harvest trip. Whew!

Two of our May prison services were unusual. On the 17th I went with Bill Glass to Noble Correctional and Belmont Correctional. Along with his usual platform guests, nine motorcyclists from Holmes County also went in, roared around the yard, and then just hung around their motorcycles and struck up conversations with curious prisoners. They then invited them to the two services that were held outside that day. It turned out to be a great day for the prisoners and for our volunteers. Then on the 23rd, Randy Keim and I went to the Federal Prison in Elkton, OH, and held a service in Spanish for about 100 inmates from ten different Spanish-speaking countries. They actually understood us! *Cristo es el Senor!*

Whether the harvest is wheat or souls of men, it won't come into the barn by itself. The farmer and the Lord both need workers for the harvest. Someone has to go out and bring in what was planted. Pray for Adam and me these next six weeks. Pray that as we bring in the harvest that I will be refreshed, renewed, and re-excited about the real harvest: people. Maybe we can harvest more than just wheat while we're working in the fields. Jesus said to His disciples, "Open your eyes and look at the fields. They are ripe for harvest" (John 4:35 NIV).

THE GRADUATE

I told the graduates at Faith Christian Academy that January 18, 1985, is burned into my memory, just as if it were yesterday. That was the day our son, Adam, was born. Now, 18-1/2 years later, that little miracle baby will graduate from Central Christian High School. Little by little I'm beginning to understand what the old folks mean when they tell us, "Time flies. They grow up fast." It's been a great ride. Our children have been such a joy to us (well, except for a day or two here and there). God has given them health, happiness, talent, financial means, and opportunities that hopefully they will use to serve God and mankind. Pray for Adam as he seeks God's will for his life.

June - 2003

THE HARVEST
(PART ONE)

We're back from the harvest! Adam graduated on June 1 and the next day he and I headed for Texas to begin the six-week furlough/father-son time/graduation present of following the wheat harvest. We got to Crowell, TX, at 7:00 am on June 3 and started cutting wheat that afternoon. Then rain shut us down for a couple of days and we played catch-up for the next ten days, trying to get the local harvest in so we could get to Thomas, OK, where the farmers were calling, "Where are you? Our wheat is ready!"

This idea all started a couple of years ago when I realized that my children were growing up and were going to graduate and leave the nest. I decided I would do something special with each one after graduation. Adam and I considered a white water rafting trip, but after realizing the cost, I said to Adam, "Why don't we go follow the wheat harvest and make some money instead of spending it?" Not knowing any better and trusting his father, he said, "Sounds great!"

Two weeks after starting, we were in a wheat field in Oklahoma at about 1:00 am. Adam had just driven the tractor and grain cart beside the combine, where about 300 bushels of wheat was dumped on his cart—the combines never stopped—and he was bringing it over to dump on my truck. As he drove past my window I saw his face (we had been up since 6:30 am) and how tired he was, and I said to myself, "What did I do to my son?" But he never complained, and as hard as it was, and as tired as we were some days, we both can say that the time flew by and we had a great time.

We started in Crowell, Texas, and from there we went to:

- Thomas, OK,

- Bucklin, KS,

- Beloit, KS,

- Stratton, CO,

- Holyoke, CO, (we could see Nebraska from here)

We finished cutting wheat in Amherst, CO, at 11:00 pm on July 9, and just after midnight on the 10th, we started for home—about 1,200 miles away—arriving in Benton at 9:00 pm. What a time! Six weeks of harvesting wheat. Adam drove the grain cart until he began running a combine the last week. One combine (w/ a thirty-foot header) can harvest about 250 acres in a day. Our average workday was sixteen hours, so we figure we harvested about 25,000 acres of wheat (from one to six combines in each field) for a grand total about 1,000,000 bushels! My job was mostly driving the truck from the field to the elevator. I drove the semi truck about 8,000 miles to twelve different elevators in four different states. I want to thank Joe and Lori Wenger who hired us for only half of the summer; the CGM board for granting me a sabbatical; and you, for your faithful support. I am ready to get back to my real calling, and Adam has eliminated farming from his list of possible careers.

July, August - 2003

THE HARVEST
(PART TWO)

Jesus said, "Lift up your eyes and look on the fields; for they are white already to harvest."

(JOHN 4:35)

Last month I wrote about what Adam and I did on the harvest. This month I want to share some spiritual insights from the wheat harvest. In fact, if you hear me preach in the next month or two, bring this letter with you and you won't have to take notes.

The Urgency of the Harvest: In every community where we worked, there was a sense of urgency. High school and college students were working at the elevators for the two-week period of the harvest. No matter what time of day I pulled in with my truck, there they were, bleary-eyed, dirty, dust masks on their faces, but they were right there, guiding us over the dump augers, unloading our trucks. The weather was on everyone's mind. Police and the local sheriff were present in every town because the truck and farm traffic was multiplied. Even though they had to know that ninety percent of the trucks were overweight and many drivers likely did not have the proper license, they simply kept order; the most important thing was not legislature, but the harvest! The farmer's whole year's wages are in those trucks. The community's economic well-being is wrapped up in the harvest. Everything takes a back seat in each community for about two weeks for the Harvest!

Harvest Time is Hard Work: Our average workday was sixteen hours! It wasn't hard physical work like I remember on the farm, but it was steady and we worked "while it was day" and even while it was dark. We had a short time to get the wheat in and we worked until it was too damp, or until the elevator closed and all the trucks, combines, and the grain cart were full of wheat, or until mechanical breakdown.

Some Fields Aren't Ready: At times the wheat was green or just not quite ripe. We had to leave it for some other harvester, because we had other customers up north who were calling and saying, "Our wheat is ready! Where are you?"

God Gives the Increase: This was a bumper crop year. The first Tuesday we were in Bucklin, KS, the local elevator owner told us that more wheat came into the seven elevators in that area that one day than came in all of last year! The same fields, same farmers, same seed, same methods; totally different results. What made the difference? God. OK, it was the weather, but God controls that, so what I'm saying is we need to sow the seed and cultivate the fields, but the results are still up to God.

You May Lose Some: From the field to the combine, from the combine to the grain cart, from the grain cart to the truck, and then to the elevator, the train car, and the silos of the flour mills, some grain is lost. Every transfer leaves little traces or piles of grain on the ground. In the spiritual harvest, some will be lost. Even Jesus lost one out of 12.

Wheat is the Same All Over the World: I started keeping a journal of our six-week tour of duty, but I noticed after ten days that every entry was the same: got up, ate breakfast, greased up my truck, cut wheat, hauled wheat, got in late. The heart of man is the same in Kansas, Oklahoma, Okinawa, India, Africa, Brazil... We all want love and acceptance, and everywhere, the deepest need of our hearts is God!

The Joy: As I look back on just six weeks (the rest of the crew is still working—they're in Montana now) I remember the tiredness, the hard work, the late nights and early mornings, but most of all I have a feeling of accomplishment, contentment, and joy! The Psalmist says, "Those who sow in tears will reap with songs of joy" (Psalms 126:5 NIV).

September - 2003

A TRIBUTE TO JOHNNY CASH
1932 - 2003

Johnny Cash died on Sept. 12, 2003. The world lost one of the most defining entertainers of the twentieth century—the Man in Black.

I believe that only my dad, my high school coach, Chuck Cargill, and Jesus have influenced my life more than Johnny Cash. The first record I ever bought was *Johnny Cash at Folsom Prison.* I was eighteen at the time and not much into music. But I liked Johnny Cash. Maybe it was because he was the first singer who seemed to be a real man. Maybe it was because he was the first singer I could sing along with. My voice never fit in. My grade school music teacher didn't have much hope for me. Maybe it was that his songs actually said something. Maybe it was the fact that I had purchased the first record in recording history to be recorded live. Whatever it was, it made me want to sing.

In the late sixties, I watched the Johnny Cash Show on TV and many times he ended the program with a gospel song. I believe I am a Christian today partly because of that. The first record I bought was recorded in a prison, and Cash's compassion for prisoners comes through the vinyl. I believe I am in prison ministry partly through his influence. I am known as a singer, largely because of Johnny Cash. My method of guitar playing, my format for concerts, banquets, churches... all have his fingerprints.

He had a remarkable career spanning half a century. He is the only person to be elected to the Country Music Hall of Fame, the Rock & Roll Hall of Fame, and the Nashville Songwriters Hall of Fame. I was in first grade when I first heard his "Ballad of a Teenage Queen." I had just graduated from high school in 1967 when his 1956 hit, "Folsom Prison Blues," hit the charts again, this time going to number one. He had fourteen number one hits and over 137 top-ten hits in his career. He recorded an amazing 1,500 songs on close to 150 albums! At the time of his death, he was up for four Grammy nominations. He never quit. He finished strong.

When he was first my hero, he wasn't a good role model. I didn't know it at the time, but he was a drug addict and he was about to go through a divorce; his life was a mess. I just liked his singing. But in 1968 he recommitted his life to Christ. By the time of his death, he was one of the most admired men in America, friend of presidents and prisoners, philanthropist and philosopher, entertainer and advocate, an overcomer and a victor. I may not have picked the right hero, but he became the right one: a real man, a true American, a struggling Christian who never quit, a man who finished strong. He is now with Jesus and reunited with his wife.

Thank you, Johnny, for all you gave me. I will miss you. I lost a friend. Because of your influence, I will keep on singing. I hope to be an overcomer, a crusader, and I plan to finish strong. I'm a better person because of your influence. I'll see you on the far banks of the Jordan.

IDOL OR HERO? *(WRITTEN PREVIOUSLY)*

It was a real thrill to meet Johnny Cash when he was in Sugarcreek. I was showing someone his picture and the question was asked, "Is he your idol?" I guess I had never thought of it before, but the way it was asked, I actually recoiled and said an emphatic, "No!" I haven't had a lot of heroes, but Johnny Cash is one person I have copied in many ways. I sing his songs; my style is patterned after his; I began to search for God after hearing his testimony; I am in prison ministry partly because of his influence. But an idol?

According to Webster's dictionary, an idol is; 1. *an image worshiped as a god. 2. a false god. 3. an object of passionate devotion.* Movie stars and singers are often called idols, and the sad truth is that they probably are. They are worshiped as God by misled and empty people.

The recent death of Jerry Garcia of the Grateful Dead brought much media attention. In several interviews with fans, it was revealed that some had been to as many as eighty-five of his concerts. He was an idol. They worshiped him (by their own admission). One person said, "Now that Jerry's gone, I don't know what I'm going to do." The Bible is very clear on idol worship. "You shall not make for yourself an idol."

hero; n. 1. a mythological or legendary figure of great strength or ability. 2. a man admired for his achievements and qualities. 3. the chief male character in a literacy or dramatic work.

I have a hero. A man that I admire for his achievements and qualities. I like Johnny Cash's singing. It was a thrill to be near him. I don't worship him, but I do emulate him and imitate him in many ways. We need heroes. Men and women whose lives are worth emulating (copying). Jesus said that when men see our good works, they should be motivated to glorify our Father in heaven. A hero inspires us to do something; to be all we can be. A hero points us to God. An idol takes the adoration for itself. An idol takes and does not give.

Yes, I have a hero. But no idols.

October - 2003

GOD IS AWESOME!

I could tell you that this newsletter is late because I was so busy (which I was) or because the printer messed up (it didn't) or we had guests (we did), but here's the reason: I couldn't think of anything to say. I thought my last three letters were so good and thought-provoking and they all came so easy; just me sharing experiences and thoughts. But this month I was blank. I had brain-lock; empty head syndrome... until I got the following letter from an inmate in Maryland where I was with Steve Wingfield. I'm still blank, so I'll let Rico start this letter with his impression of a chapel service:

Dear Evangelist Schmid;

On Sunday, October 5, 2003, at the 7:30 and 11:45 am Non-Denominational Services here at Eastern Correctional Institution [Maryland], we were blessed to have you and the other volunteers come and share with us in the spirit of our Lord and Savior Jesus Christ. We were very pleased to have you, and God's message was well received. But I must tell you, this will be one to share with my Grandchildren in the years to come. Just imagine, a white man from Ohio, singing Country Western style Gospel music to a predominately black prison inmate population (smile). As I scanned the room, I noticed Brothers looking over their shoulders to see if anyone had noticed their toes tapping and fingers stumping the chair in front of them. "God is Awesome!"

We thank God for you, giving Him all Praise, Honor, and Glory. You witnessed and demonstrated to us that you're a willing vessel obedient to God's calling on your life. Brother, may God continue to bless you and use you in His service until He returns to take us home.

– RICO

BANQUET REPORT

Our Fall Banquet turned out to be a great time of food, fellowship, entertainment, information, and inspiration. In addition to you coming and showing your support, we had World Champion basketball handler Tanya Crevier for the second time in two years. She happened to be in the area and offered to come.

Since she works with Bill Glass Prison Ministries, we called fellow volunteer Ron Kuntz from Cleveland, a world-class photographer who shared some of his experiences in prison. He said he had covered the last twenty Super Bowls, many Olympics, World Series, and all the Indians games, but none of that even compares to the thrill of leading someone to Jesus in prison.

Larry Skant, an ex-offender we met while he was incarcerated, gave an update of how he is doing since he was released last year, and Sam Bender, ex-Major League Baseball Chaplain and Bill Glass's first prison director, opened the meeting in prayer. My good friend pastor Jerry Durham (who goes to a lot of banquets) said, "This is the best banquet I have ever attended!" On top of that great compliment, we raised over $5,000 for the ministry! Thank you.

Happy Thanksgiving!

1 Thessalonians 5:18

November – 2003

HOME FOR CHRISTMAS

Four years ago I asked an inmate to give his thoughts on spending Christmas in prison.

> In 1992, my first Christmas in prison, almost any reminder of the season would bring tears of sadness and heartache to my life. Attending church services was particularly hard and I found it impossible to sing Christmas carols without becoming choked up. The one thing that helped was the many holiday greetings I received. December is the toughest time for us in prison...

That inmate is now home and will be spending Christmas with his family this year.

What is it about Christmas that makes us want to be home? Why are "I'll be Home for Christmas" and "I'm Dreaming of a White Christmas" two of the best-selling songs of our time? Christmas is not even the most important day in the Christian calendar. Easter, the resurrection of Christ, is the event that changed history and brought us salvation. The early church didn't think that the anniversary of the birth of Christ was important enough to celebrate until AD 336. Even then, it was to replace an existing pagan holiday, which featured worship of the sun. The Roman god Saturnalia, or "sun," was supposedly born on December 25, and some early Christians would actually turn around and bow to the sun before entering a church. Christian leaders began to rebuke them: "The sun was not born; it was created by God. The Son was born!" And so we now celebrate the birth of the Son.

Interestingly, Jesus is the Light of the world, and without Him we cannot live. Many of the pagan practices, such as lighting candles and giving gifts, were already part of the culture, so it was easy to use the same customs to point the pagans and Christians to Jesus. So, even though December 25 is probably not the exact day of the birth of the Son, it has become the biggest celebration in the Christian year. Many people, including me, want nothing more than to be home with my family on Christmas.

Could it be that we were born to worship God, and we are restless until we do what we were created for? Could it be that we cannot do what we were created for until the Son of God is born in our hearts? He has gone to prepare a place for us (Heaven) and wants us to spend eternity with Him there (home). Could it be that Christmas symbolizes all this and gives us an inner desire to be home?

I said all that to say this: I hope you will be home for Christmas!

Merry Christmas!

December - 2003

HAPPY AD 2004!

(AD - ANNO DOMINI, IN THE YEAR OF OUR LORD)

Another year has come and gone. I am writing this on New Year's Eve, 2003, and either I am getting old or just tired of being busy (or both), but I am looking forward to a boring evening tonight. If all goes according to plan, I will be sleeping when 2004 arrives.

"The harvest is past, the summer is ended, and we are not saved" (Jeremiah 8:20 NIV).

The new year is a great time for reflection and planning, looking back at what worked and why, and planning ahead to see how we can do even better. It's like halftime at a football game. The coach draws X's and O's on a board, trying to explain what we did in the first half and how it worked, and here's what we can do in the second half to give us a better chance of scoring and keeping the other team from moving the ball.

This verse from Jeremiah takes on new meaning for me after working for a custom harvester for six weeks last summer. After every field of wheat there was an evaluation, not only to figure out how much to charge the farmer, but the farmer wanted to know if it was worth fertilizing, did he sow seed at the right time, did it pay to irrigate, how could he improve the yield next year...?

The harvest is past, the summer is ended... most of us think we have plenty of time, but this past year I lost many friends and acquaintances to death. For many of them, it was unexpected. In your planning for 2004, make sure you are saved, ready to go if the harvester should show up unexpectedly. May God grant you a wonderful AD 2004!

January - 2004

WHAT A MESS!

I again had the privilege to sing with the Inspirations at their annual Haiti benefit concert at Bahia Vista Mennonite Church in Sarasota, FL. (They closed for me again.) I left the next day to be a part of the We Care Prison Revival in Atmore, AL. Just before I got to Montgomery, I stopped to fuel up and I met a couple at the diesel pump. They asked what I do and when I told them I am involved in prison ministry, the man said he has a brother in a certain prison—could I look him up and tell him to call home?

I went to that prison and I was able to make contact with the brother. He came to chapel. I went over and introduced myself and called him by name and told him I had met his brother. He was pleasantly surprised. He said his last few calls had been refused so he thought his brother didn't want to talk to him. He was glad to hear the invitation to call. After the service there was some kind of irregularity in the prison, so we were confined to the chapel for an extra three hours. It gave me a chance to hear Joe's story. One of the basic rules for prison ministry is to never ask a prisoner why he is in. But every now and then a man will volunteer his story. Here is Joe's:

> I came home from work one night and my wife seemed distressed. When I asked what was wrong, she said a mutual friend had come over and forced himself on her. I got my shotgun and went to see this man. When confronted, the "friend" confessed that he and my wife had been intimate, but it was consensual and he paid her for it. He then went into his bedroom and closed the door and I thought he was getting a gun so I shot through the door, hitting him in the face. Then in my rage, I set his bed on fire and left.
>
> That night the police came to my place and arrested me and took me to jail. Later, while I was out on bail, my wife confessed that the relationship had been consensual, that she did it so she could get more money for drugs (we were both on drugs, even though I had my

own construction company and was doing well financially) and she hoped I would kill him so I wouldn't find out the truth (he was not seriously injured). I got charged with attempted murder and arson, forty-five years on each count. I am serving ninety years.

Joe went on to say that his wife has since remarried (she needed to move on with her life) and he only sees his two boys once a month when his mother comes to visit. In the hour or so that we talked during the lockdown, he did say that one good thing that happened is that he committed his life to Jesus. "That might make it worth it all," he said.

What a mess! Joe is right. If he found Jesus, it is worth it all... but what a cost! He could have found Jesus while he was in the free world. He would have found that he didn't need the drugs, his wife wouldn't have felt the need to get money at any cost and then lie about it; he would still have his construction company and be contributing $25,000 a year to Christian causes instead of costing the taxpayer that much. Solomon was wise to say, "Remember your Creator in the days of your youth, before the days of trouble come..." (Ecclesiastes 12:1 NIV).

February - 2004

COSTA RICA & FLORIDA REPORT

What a month! We took a two-week mission trip to Costa Rica with ten enthusiastic short-term missionaries from Church of the Savior in Wooster! After they painted, mimed, and preached in a little village for a week, they left for home on February 7. Adam, Katie, and I stayed until the 11th, visiting friends and doing some ministry. I sang and spoke at several places and we saw many old (or should I say, long time) friends and some of our former youth.

Adam had two firsts in these four days: He sang by himself with a guitar for the English-speaking youth group of San Jose! (He's sung many times with the family, but never by himself.) The next day on the way to Talamanca, he got his first traffic violation! He has driven in the States for three years and has never been stopped. He drove ten minutes in Costa Rica and got pulled over by the police! *"Muy rapido!"* ("Very fast!") was the policeman's greeting. They let him go because he couldn't understand them and he looked so innocent. We visited the church in Carbon that we had helped build about five years ago. Katie got to visit Marta, the girl she stayed with in 1997.

Back at home, after minister's fellowship in Berlin and a concert in Daviess County, IN, Lydia and I took off for Florida to be a part of the Gospel Express Benefit Auction in Sarasota. It is always great to be a part of Nelson Coblentz's ministry and also to see all of our friends in Florida from around the country. We even saw Mr. and Mrs. Bob Wilmarth, a missionary couple on furlough from Costa Rica! I sang somewhere every day I was there.

One of the highlights was singing at the Tabernacle (church) on Sunday morning where Lydia's cousin Barbara Barwick attends. The guest speaker that morning was Bruce Collie, a former NFL player with the 49ers. He and his wife and their ten (yes, 10) children presented the gospel. I had known Bruce from working with Bill Glass. Tino Wallenda, the famous circus high wire performer and his family, also attend there, and he invited Lydia and me to the circus that afternoon. He said, "Just come to the entrance and tell them Tino sent you and ask for Chuck." So, we did. (Just like the Kingdom of God; it's who you know!) We had reserved seats to watch Tino and his family perform one of the most famous circus acts of all time, the seven-man pyramid on a high wire thirty feet above the ground, with no safety net. It makes prison ministry look pretty safe and easy.

We are happy, busy, tired, and sore (I have a bad rotator cuff), but I am getting ready to hit the Ohio prisons this Spring. Pray with us for open doors, good health, energy, and that "whenever I speak, words may be given me so that I will fearlessly make known the mystery of the gospel..." (Ephesians 6:19).

March - 2004

A STORY FROM THE OHIO PENITENTIARY

Men are not in prison because of lack of intelligence, but lack of wisdom and morals; the wrong use of their intelligence. I was in a prison chapel in Missouri last year where there were six lawyers, three doctors, two judges, and a congressman on the first two rows! I also correspond with a man in this prison who has a Ph.D. and speaks five languages.

Here is one of ten thousand tragic stories from the 150-year history of the old Ohio State Penitentiary, which closed in 1984. It is an excerpt from "Motive," published by the Ohio Department of Mental Hygiene and Correction.

In 1898, a Texas federal judge sentenced William Sidney Porter to five years in the Ohio Penitentiary for embezzlement. This unknown thirty-three-year-old alcoholic bookkeeper emerged from obscurity three years later to become one of the world's best-known authors... O. Henry.

It seems that Porter would sit alone in his cell and write. One of his first stories, "The Gift of the Magi," became a Christmas classic, and after that, his stories literally poured out from behind the prison walls. To this day, no one knows how Porter managed to smuggle his manuscripts out of prison. The story with the most credence says that he sent them to the relative of a fellow prisoner who then forwarded them to a publisher. Porter did not sign his real name to any of his works. He used the pseudonym, O. Henry, under the title of each story.

Porter, inmate #30664, worked in the prison hospital. He was discharged after serving three years, two months, and twenty-seven days of his five-year sentence. No one knew then that the prison recreation yard would someday be named in his honor... O. Henry field.

Porter left Ohio and went to New York. He continued to write until he again fell under the influence of alcohol. Twelve years after his discharge from the Ohio Penitentiary, Porter was found dead on the fringes of New York's skid row. The world mourned the death of one of its favorite authors. Old stories say that he had twenty-three cents in his pocket. The medical report stated that the cause of death was cirrhosis of the liver... caused by alcohol.

What a sad ending! Here was a man who went to prison because he was stealing money to support his addiction. He became one of the most loved authors in the world and then went right back to prison, not a prison with walls and bars, but a prison of addiction that took his life while he was still in his 40's. That addiction robbed the world of who knows how many more great works of literature that were hidden in his creative heart.

If only William Sidney Porter (O. Henry) had heeded the advice of one of the wisest men who ever lived: "Remember your Creator in the days of your youth, before the days of trouble come, and the years approach when you will say, 'I find no pleasure in them'" (Ecclesiastes 12:1 NIV).

April - 2004

A LETTER FROM PRISON

Dear Mr. Schmid,

Greetings in the name of our Lord and Savior, Jesus Christ. I've always wanted to write and tell you about how much I've enjoyed your singing and the programs that you put on for us here at ACI, but I kept getting side tracked, but after you sang "Long Black Train" recently I decided that I shouldn't put it off any longer, for I was deeply moved by your version of it just as I was a few years ago when I sat in the back of the chapel and heard you sing the T. Graham Brown song, "Wine Into Water." As a matter of fact, I was so moved by it that I wrote Mr. Brown and he sent me an autographed picture, which I proudly display next to the pictures of George Jones and my pen pal, Jeff Foxworthy.

Anyway, this isn't about my autograph collection, but it is about a man named Jesus Christ and what He's doing through you, you're such a blessing and inspiration and you give hope to those who have very little by reaching out and reminding us that we're not alone.

As for my personal story, I'd like to share a little bit of it with you. Mr. Schmid, on the streets I was the world's biggest loser. My life style was sinful, I drank every day and was on my way to hell, but I didn't care because the drugs and the alcohol had control of my life. They numbed my brain, distorted the reality of truth and made the ride to hell a lot smoother, but for some unknown reason in the fall of '96 my world began to fall apart. The ride to hell got faster and I began to face tragedy after tragedy and I even attempted suicide, but God had other plans. By April of '97, I found myself facing prison for a crime, which I didn't commit. I was again considering taking my own life, because the years of drinking and drugging had begun to take their toll on me. As I began to dry out I began to hear voices, so with what was left of my shattered mind I cried out to God and He heard me. After

I prayed the sinner's prayer I was set free in ways that I'd never known before.

Mr. Schmid, if this had happened to someone else I would've accused them of exaggerating, because the Lord has moved in my life in ways that I never thought possible. Not only has He removed the desires of drinking and drugging, but a few years ago He blessed me with a song and gave me two very good friends, Steve & Annie Chapman. Steve & I co-wrote his song, "He Never Did Anything," which is on their CD, *This House Still Stands*. Steve also mentions the song and my innocence in his book, *With God on A Deer Hunt* and he's also made a couple of trips to ACI to sing for us...

Well, that's my story and I'm glad to share it with you, something I rarely do. As for the song, "He Never Did Anything," most of the inmates here already know that I helped to write it, so I hope that someday you'll learn it and sing it for us, for I really like the way you sing. You are a blessing and a comfort. God bless you.

Note: I received this letter last Fall. I got my copy of *This House Still Stands* and sure enough, Steve Chapman sings a song, "He Never Did Anything", written by James Alley. These words are inside the cover:

One day I picked up my mail and in the stack of letters was an envelope from a prison in Lima, Ohio. In it was a letter and poem from Mr. James Alley. His note was encouraging and the verses he sent gripped my heart. I wrote back and asked him if I could develop it into a song. In the finished work, I hope you can hear the cry of a heart that has come to understand the crime committed to Christ—the Innocent Lamb.

– STEVE

This letter reinforces several of my philosophies of life: Ninety percent of ministry is simply showing up, there is power in a song, there is talent behind prison bars, and the system is a monster. Although everyone in prison claims to be innocent, some actually are.

By the way, I do sing his song, "He Never Did Anything." The two songs he mentions, "Long Black Train" and "Wine Into Water" are on my new recording, *What a Time.*

May - 2004

COSTA RICA & FLORIDA REPORT

For a Christian, the answer to "What causes crime?" is simple; sin. James says, Does [crime] not come from your desires for pleasure that war in your members? You lust and do not have. You murder and covet and cannot obtain. You fight and war. Yet you do not have...

Man has been looking for solutions to crime since time began. The first murder is recorded in the fourth chapter of Genesis. Cain, the first person to be born on planet Earth, killed his own brother, Abel. Motive: jealousy. Ever since sin entered the world through disobedience, man's desire has not been to please God, but to please himself, and this results in a society that needs policemen, courtrooms, prisons, and all sorts of crime prevention. It is interesting to hear some of the explanations of why there is crime.

In his history book on the Ohio Penitentiary, James C. Ridpath wrote this about the cause of crime:

> I asked a preacher what was the cause of crime and he said it was original sin and nothing more. I asked a doctor and he said it was bad health, that crime is only a form of disease. I asked a lawyer and he said, defining a circle, that it was the violation of the law and he would attend to it. He gave me his card. I asked a banker and he said it was the silver agitation. The Silverites had destroyed public confidence. I asked a teacher and he said it was the lack of education, the ignorance of the masses. I asked an astronomer and he said it was the spots on the sun. I asked a biologist and he said crime is zymotic in its origin with bacillus. I asked a politician and he said it was the essential badness of the law. He was a candidate for the lower house. I asked a busy man and he said it was indolence, that idleness is the mother of all vice. I asked a nurseryman and he said it was the lack of fruit. I asked a man who had a phonetic alphabet and he said it was the abomination of the English orthography.

I agree with the preacher in the article above. That is why I focus on going into prisons with a message of the gospel of Jesus Christ. The Bible says, "If anyone is in Christ, he is a new creation; old things have passed away, behold, all things have become new." If this statement in 2 Corinthians 5:17 were not true, I would be pretty stupid to go to prisons. I have missed family events and school activities, and have spent thousands of dollars to go to prison chapels. But that statement is true, and therefore I have the audacity to go into a prison chapel where there are men who have committed horrible atrocities, and I tell them that Jesus can change their lives! That's good news! That's what the gospel is: good news.

Although there have been many disappointments, I have seen men whose lives have been dramatically changed through a relationship with Christ. Men full of hatred and bitterness, blame and guilt, have been changed into men with compassion, love, freedom, and a desire to reach out and help rather than reach out and take. Yes, crime is a sin problem and the only One who can change that is the One who died to take away our sin. Jesus is the answer!

June - 2004

AN ENCOUNTER AT AN ENCOUNTER

"Number 13... number 13..." The man at the hamburger joint in Franklin, WV, had a blank look on his unshaven face as he held Bruce Hummel's hamburger on a tray and unenthusiastically repeated, "Number 13..." (Bruce often flies me to places–at his expense–when my schedule gets crowded. On this particular day I had a wedding in the morning and a Wingfield Encounter in the evening.) I know you can't judge a book by its cover, but I found myself pitying this hamburger man in his 60's who obviously had missed out on the great American dream. Flipping hamburgers is near the bottom of the economic food chain (no pun intended). But, at least he was working. Most of the people I deal with are in prison because they take shortcuts to avoid work, or take drugs to forget about the everydayness of work.

Since Bruce was out of eyeshot at the drink dispenser, the man looked at me blankly and said, "What's your name?"

"John," I said.

"I thought so," he replied. "You stayed at my house in Bermuda."

Mistaken identity, I thought! This man? In Bermuda? But, how did he know I had once been there on mission/concert tour? Since I didn't know what else to say,

I said, "What's your name?"

"Dan Jolly," he said.

Sure enough! That was the name of the folks I had stayed with when I was in Bermuda in 1980 (24 years ago!). I couldn't believe it!

"You're bigger." he said. The overweight girls working with him thought that was a terrible thing to say, but it was true.

Twenty-four years ago Dan was a big shot at the Naval base in Bermuda. He lived in a beautiful house. And now here he is flipping burgers! So, we exchanged pleasantries and asked how each other was doing, but deep down I'm wondering, "What happened to Dan?" He must have fallen on hard times somewhere along the line. When he went to the back of the kitchen, I asked the girl at the cash register about him. "Dan? Oh, he's a big shot at the Naval base outside of town. He just works here for kicks. He enjoys meeting people who don't know his high rank in the navy," she said.

I was amazed, intrigued, a little embarrassed at my attitude, and pleasantly surprised that someone who knew me for just ten days recognized me after so long. (We long to be recognized.) I didn't get a chance to ask Dan why he works at a fast food place, but I have thought about our chance meeting many times in the last three weeks. I was reminded that you really can't judge a book by its cover. I wonder, how many people do we meet throughout the day who get tired of being known for their position or rank and just want to be known for the person they are? I suppose some people only have rank and don't really want to expose their real selves. I wonder how many people I write off as losers because of the job they are performing. I may have written off Jesus because He was doing a job that was considered lower than a burger flipper when He washed the disciple's feet. James 2:9 warns us, "If you show favoritism, you sin..."

It was good to see Dan after twenty-four years. It was good to be reminded that our worth is not based on our position or rank. God loves us all equally and I should strive to be like Him in that respect, whether I'm dealing with prince or pauper, king or janitor, banker or burger flipper, policeman or prisoner. Be aware the next time you go buy a burger. The man behind the counter may ask you your name.

July - 2004

IT'S WHO YOU KNOW

I was traveling on I-71 from Cleveland to Mansfield with Bill Glass prison ministries when I got a cell phone call from son Adam, who was scheduled to fly home from Costa Rica that day with our church youth group. "You're in Miami!" I said. "No, we're still in San Jose," he replied. "They won't let Amy on the plane!"

"What? Why?!" I asked. He said, "Because she is a minor and since she was born in Costa Rica, she is a citizen and is under Costa Rican law, so she needs her parents signature to leave the country!"

Talk about a bad day! I was on the road and Lydia was at home with visiting relatives. I immediately called my friend Ron Ross (these cell phones are amazing!) who lives in San Jose but was vacationing in Colorado. He said, "You've got a problem!" He called his neighbor in Costa Rica who is second-in-command of the Alajuela Patronato (children's services) and told him the situation. He said, "Big problem!" Then I called the Costa Rican consulate in Chicago, the US embassy in Costa Rica... then I realized I probably should call Lydia. She immediately called Buddy Roberts, a friend in Costa Rica who knows everybody. He said, "Oh my, big problem! But I'll see what I can do."

By this time our prison team had arrived at the Richland Correctional Institution, so I went in with the fifty-some volunteers and did my part in the program and tried not to worry about Amy and Adam. (Right!) When I finally got out at 4:00 pm (we entered at noon), I called Lydia. She said, "Amy got on the plane! It was a miracle!" (Actually, she and Adam got a plane, the next one to Miami, but it was still a miracle.)

They were stuck in Miami overnight but stayed with missionary friends, Kevin Jezequels. They got home Saturday at 5:00 pm, instead of 9:00 pm on Friday the 23rd.

From what we can piece together, Ron Ross's friend in Costa Rica, Jorge Sanabria, called the US Embassy and the Patronato de Alajuela and the airlines. He also called a lawyer friend who made some calls and also put together a document saying that Amy has her parent's permission to leave the country. He called the airlines to get Amy's passport number and they couldn't release it because of the privacy act. So he called a high government official who called the airlines and they released her passport number in spite of the privacy act! Then he presented his document to the Patronato de Alajuela who presented it to the immigration officials and the airport.

Buddy Roberts called some influential friends in the government who began calling the embassy and the airlines. The response that all of these folks got was, "Yes, we are aware of the case." In other words, "Who is this girl? She must be somebody important to be getting calls from the patronato, the government, several lawyers, and Buddy Roberts!" Although we think the clincher was Jorge Sanabria's document, we know that several immigration officials and airline workers met a young girl with lots of friends!

Absent in this story are all the prayer chains that were activated. Since that would take another whole page to tell, suffice it to say that even with all wonderful help of all the above-mentioned people, God was the One who released Amy! She is now safely home with us. Our God is an awesome God! Oh yes, and they had a great mission trip!

August - 2004

BE YOURSELF

Sometimes I wonder what the prisoners are thinking. I'm up front singing country gospel style songs and a large portion of the congregation is African American or Hispanic. The rest are white, and half of them are not country music fans. So, what do I do? Well, I sing country gospel style songs! That's who I am. I used to be intimidated when I realized that I was singing to a "non-country" audience, but I have learned that one thing prisoners dislike more than someone who is not their style is someone who is a fake. When I tried to "become all things to all men..." by singing different styles, the result was less than authentic. The best way to be real is to be real. In almost every prison service there is much appreciation shown for the message that comes through the songs, even though the style is not their own. (Once I sang "I've Been Everywhere" at a Bill Glass prison weekend and a black brother said, "Man, that's Hillbilly Rap"!) My advice? Imitate and emulate the great singers and preachers, but in the end, be yourself. Nobody can do that quite like you can!

CATCHING UP (OR, MORE NEWS)

This past month I have had the opportunity to sing country style in quite a few different settings: a 100th birthday party; the Mennonite Relief auction; a trail ride; a lunch for senior citizens; a fundraising meal; a small town homecoming; a restaurant; a campground; a business picnic; several churches, and about seven prison services. In each setting I was myself. (I'm pretty good at that.) The message transcends the style, and even in secular settings, I was able to communicate the love of Jesus.

On the 21st of August, I had the opportunity to sing "He Never Did Anything" at a prison service. James Alley, the man who wrote the song, was in attendance (I told his story in my May newsletter). It was good to finally meet him face to face after singing his song in prisons all across Ohio since last December. I think he was pleased with my rendition of his song.

NEW SECRETARY
Bonita Yoder is the new secretary for Common Ground Ministries. She is the daughter of Earl and Effie Beachy of Berlin and is married to Dean Yoder, who is originally from Kalona, IA. Welcome, Bonita!

September - 2004

LONDON FREEDOM RALLY
Common Ground Ministries teamed up with The Gospel Echoes and stormed London Prison, OH, with almost 150 volunteers on Friday, September 24! Thirty-some folks from Wayne and Holmes Counties, along with over 100 people from the Plain City area, went in armed with barbeque grills, hamburgers, potato salad, Bibles, aprons, smiles, etc., and served 2,000 inmates a meal like they haven't had since they

landed in prison (except those who were there two years ago when we did the same thing). We also handed out 1,700 New Testaments to the inmates as they left the meal (not everyone accepted one). The volunteers personally served the meal in the main mess hall and then went around and refilled the soft drinks (unheard of in prison).

That night we had the first of eight services outside in the main yard, with singing and preaching. Not quite 200 men were seated in front of the stage, but with the sound system, almost everyone in the yard could hear the singing and preaching. During the actual service, volunteers were able to mingle with the men in the yard as they played basketball, lifted weights, jogged, etc., and engage them in conversation.

Although there were decisions in every service, many others stated how they would never be the same after hearing a certain song or sermon (but they would never come close enough to the stage to appear that they were listening). The Gospel Echoes and I shared the singing schedule. Glendon Bender, Todd Neuschwander, Jim Eigsti, and I preached, not only on the main yard, but in the camp next door to the prison. Here are some of the comments:

"I haven't felt like a human being since I got locked up two years ago, until yesterday, when someone came and refilled my drink at supper."

"The mess hall is never this quiet and peaceful."

"Even the dorms are more peaceful since you've been here."

"Now I know that somebody out there cares."

"Thanks for coming. You give us hope."

"I dedicated my life to Christ today."

A special thanks to the following for donating the Bibles for this special weekend: Glen Graber, Bill & Eva Keim, Bennie Mast, Willie Mast, Myrl Nofziger, Dwain Schlabach, Levi Troyer, and Mennonite Christian Assembly.

October - 2004

PROMISES

During this time of the year I have to think about promises. God's promises are precious and real and we can take them to the bank; we can base our lives on them. On the other hand, I have heard some outlandish promises during this political campaign, from economic prosperity to healing folks with spinal injuries. I was reminded of Pepe Figueres, the hero of the Costa Rican revolution in 1948, a great man, but also a politician. During a campaign stop in the early '50s at a remote pueblo with no roads, Don Pepe promised the people a bridge so the highway could come to their town. When nobody cheered like he thought they should, an aide came on stage and whispered in his ear, "Don Pepe, they don't need a bridge. There is no river here." Pepe didn't miss a beat in the rhythm of his speech, "... and... I also promise a river!"

Elton Yutzy from Plain City tells this story about political promises:

It was election time and a politician decided to go out to the local reservation and try to get the Native

American vote. They were all assembled in the Council Hall to hear the speech. The politician had worked up to his finale, and the crowd was getting more and more excited. "I promise better education opportunities for Native Americans!" The crowd went wild, shouting *"Hoya! Hoya!"* The politician was a bit puzzled by the native word but was encouraged by their enthusiasm. "I promise gambling reforms to allow a Casino on the Reservation!" *"Hoya! Hoya!"* cried the crowd, stomping their feet. "I promise more social reforms and job opportunities for Native Americans!" The crowd reached a frenzied pitch shouting *"Hoya! Hoya! Hoya!"* After the speech, the politician was touring the reservation and saw a tremendous herd of cattle. Since he was raised on a ranch and knew a bit about cattle, he asked the Chief if he could get closer to take a look at the cattle. "Sure," the Chief said, "but be careful not to step in the hoya."

By the time you receive this, the election will be over (hopefully). I have very strong feelings about which candidate will be better for our country, but I have to remind myself that in the end, only God's promises are trustworthy and life-giving. I am going to vote and pray, but in the end, my citizenship is not of this world. I was bought with a price and I am not my own. I believe St. Paul would have voted. He used his citizenship to his advantage in Acts 16. After they were beaten and put in jail (and led the jailer and his family to salvation in Jesus), the magistrates sent their officers to the jailer with orders to "release those men." Paul said, "They beat us publicly without a trial even though we are Roman citizens and threw us into prison. And now do they want to get rid of us quietly? No! Let them come themselves and escort us out!" Don't you just love Paul's boldness? The big shots came and escorted them out of the city. Later, in Acts 22, Paul was being led away to be flogged and he asked a simple question: "Is it legal for you to flog a Roman citizen who hasn't even been found guilty?"

We have rights as citizens of this country, and we also have responsibilities in a government of the people, by the people, and for the people (that's us). And by the way, if you don't vote in the final election, you lose!

In the final election, Jesus gets one vote,

Satan gets one vote, and you get one vote.

Majority wins.

Vote.

November - 2004

2005

ANNUAL SHORT-TERM MISSION TRIP

I started home at 9:30 pm from Shipshewana, IN, on Wednesday, December 22. I had been a part of Mel Riegsecker's Blue Gate Dinner Theatre for three nights and I was anxious to get home the day before Christmas Eve. It was cold and clear in Indiana, but the closer I got to Ohio the snowier it got, and by the time I got off the turnpike near Norwalk, traffic was crawling along at about 20 mph! On an interstate highway! The four-and-a-half hour trip took about eight hours. I got home at 4:30 am and saw candlelight through the windows. Lydia was up and said the electric had gone off and it was getting cold in the house. The electric didn't come back on until the 29th, six days later! With our neighbor's generator, we were able to have heat and water and a few lights, so it was an inconvenience rather than a crisis, but we were reminded of how nice we have it here in the U.S.

The day after the lights came on at home, Lydia and our two girls and I took off for Costa Rica with seventeen Central Christian students and a couple from Hartville, Lavern and Marilyn Wagler (we needed help). We went to the town of Guápiles to build a pastor's office/study for Rev. Ernesto Alvarez. We also scraped and painted the concrete walls in the Sunday School rooms of his church, and several evenings we held services in drug rehabilitation centers in town. The students would sing—they are good!—give testimonies, and then I would preach.

Pastor Alvarez is new to this town, and our presence gave him an excuse to contact the centers. Now he hopes to begin an ongoing ministry there, so our presence not only helped the physical building of his church, but it opened doors for him to go out into the community. (90 percent of ministry is showing up.) After a week of hard work, we went to the beach for two days of rest and relaxation, only to be participants in the worst tropical rainstorm to hit Costa Rica in thirty-five years! It rained hard all night (and this is dry season!), so we decided to go back to San Jose for our second day of debriefing. We were delayed and detoured by high water and washed-out bridges, but we made it back to the capital by nightfall. The next morning there was a small earthquake, so we feel good that the Central students got the full spectrum of Central America: a tropical storm, a flood, and an earthquake!

Pastor Ernesto had been praying for an office/study room, and he asked God to give it to him by the end of January. With the limited resources of that culture, he knew it would take a miracle, but he said he changed his theology from "seeing is believing" to "believing is seeing." He said he could see the room. And wouldn't you know, God in His wisdom prompted my daughter Amy to talk to me about taking a mini-term group to Costa Rica. Mini-term just happens to be the first weeks of January, and the project that Christ for the Cities Mission picked was Iglesia Misionera Centro Americana in Guápiles, Ernesto's church! We didn't finish the project, but by the time you read this, Ernesto will be studying, praying, and preparing sermons in the study built by students that were sent by God from a Christian school 2,200 miles away at just the right time. (You financed some of them.) It feels good to be the answer to someone's prayers.

Not only were lives changed at the rehabilitation centers, but after the first service, new missionary Joe Yoder led one of the Central students in a prayer of Salvation!

January, February - 2005

THE POWER OF A RECORDED SONG

"We listen to your CD all the time! We just love it!" Those are encouraging words, especially if you're the one who recorded the CD! That was in an email from a pastor's wife near Chicago. (Country Gospel in Chicago?) She went on to say that she ordered one from our website for a young man in their church with the hopes that he would listen to it and come back to the Lord.

Every now and then I hear someone tell how one of my recordings ministered to them. A prisoner from London Correctional wrote to me several years ago and said that he gave his heart to the Lord late one night after listening to "Greystone Chapel" over and over. One of the things that touched his heart was hearing my son, Adam, who was only six years old at the time of the recording, laugh on one of the songs. Larry Skrant, who now has his own prison ministry based in Spencer, OH, said that when he got word that his dad died late one night, there was no chaplain on duty at the prison, so he went back to his cell at NCCI and listened to "This Is My Father's World." That ministered to him until the chaplain came in the next morning and he was able to make a phone call to his family. (When I sang at Larry's church last January, the organist played "This Is My Father's World," not knowing why tears were coming down Larry's face.)

One of the most surprising and gratifying reports I heard was when a friend told me that in the last days of her mother's life, about the only thing that would get a response from her mother was when they played the CD, *In Dutch!* The old German hymns and Pennsylvania Dutch songs seemed to penetrate the fog and shroud of sickness and pain and take her back to her childhood and heritage, and she would smile. Since then, several other friends have told me similar stories. What an encouragement to think that my recordings may have had a small part in alleviating someone's pain and suffering! And I almost didn't do the *In Dutch!* project because it seemed like a waste of money and time for such a frivolous recording in a German dialect with a limited audience. It has become our best seller and has opened doors all over the US and Canada!

Why am I thinking of the power of recordings right now? Probably because last month one of my songs was released on a Bobby G. Rice compilation disc. Harvey Perdue from Hot Springs, AR, heard my song "The Date" and told his Nashville friend Bobby about it. We got in touch and I sent him the song and he said, "Who knows? It might go." It's a Christian song going to 900 country music stations, but he said with so many of the modern country songs having a Christian theme, this may be the time for this song. I'm realistic enough not to get too excited, but it would be fun to have a song that speaks to thousands each time it's played, rather than several. The chances of anything happening are slim to none, but I cast my bread on the surface of the waters...

March - 2005

A CHAMPION

Six-time World Welterweight Boxing Champion! Two-time Olympic gold medalist! Financially set for life! All the security, fame, and fortune a twenty-some-year-old could want! Yes, I met Pernell (Sweet Pea) Whitaker, the World Champion boxer from Virginia who made it to the top. He had a record of 520 wins and 14 losses. He had a gold chain around his neck and gold rings on his fingers when I talked to him. He was also wearing prison clothes.

Yes, I met this world champion athlete in prison! We were in Harrisonburg, VA, for Wingfield Ministries' Spring Fest in the Valley. I was part of the prison outreach, along with Billy Graham's prison team of Dallas Anderson and Marvis Frazier.

Marvis is a boxer, the son of former heavyweight champion Smokin' Joe Frazier. Of all the people God could have chosen to speak at this event, He picked a boxer! We were in the park and about fifty inmates came from the halfway house, called Gemeinschaft, in Harrisonburg. After a barbeque picnic lunch, Marvis gave his testimony, I sang, and then Dallas Anderson gave the challenge to follow Christ. The first hand that shot up belonged to Sweet Pea. He couldn't wait for the chance to dedicate himself to something that mattered.

As Sweet Pea's story unfolded, it seems that he had everything: money, fame, material goods... everything but peace. He was totally bored with life and he turned to cocaine to fill the void and ended up in prison. Now here he was in a prison work-release program. When we first met him he had a tough guy look about him, but when we left, he was smiling. It seems the old saying has some validity: Everything minus God = Nothing. Nothing + God = Everything.

Note Webster's definition–

Cham-pi-on: n. 1. a winner. 2. a defender, advocate, or supporter of a cause or another person.

April - 2005

THEY GROW UP FAST, YEAH, YEAH...

Twenty years ago I remember writing from Costa Rica: "I am suspending all advice on how to raise children for the next eighteen years." I was a youth pastor and quite often was asked by parents how to deal with their children. I always had great, helpful advice. However, after my son, Adam, was born, I realized that I was like the man who said "I had five theories on child rearing and no children. Now I have five children and no theories." I suppose James Dobson had the best advice when he said, "Just get them through... and pray, pray, pray." He also quoted someone who said that when your child turns thirteen, put him in a barrel and feed him through the hole. When he turns sixteen, plug the hole! Of course, he was being facetious. (How do you like that five-dollar word? It means he was kidding.) The point is well taken, though, that raising children today seems to be a lot more dangerous than when we lived on farms and had work to do and no time to get into trouble.

When I was growing up we had all kinds of protection morally (modest dress, decent TV, no internet, decency laws, neighbor informants that let our parents know what we were doing), but I know many people my age or my parent's age who lost fingers or have scars because of farm or factory accidents. There wasn't as much concern for physical safety. I remember going to Wooster, sitting on the tailgate of the pickup with my feet dragging on the highway. And sometimes my dad would even strike a match without closing the cover!

Today, our physical protection is of utmost concern, but morally and spiritually we can be mortally wounded. Our society not only doesn't care, but they make it illegal to put up moral guardrails (child porn protected by first amendment, abstinence not an option, Ten Commandments outlawed, etc., ad infinitum, ad nauseam). I'm not against being safe, I just think Ralph Nader ought to get a life and some of our lawmakers ought to get a life sentence.

I said all to say that this month Adam will graduate from Rosedale Bible College and on June 5, Amy will graduate from Central Christian. By the grace of God, they have been a joy to raise, even with all of our mistakes and inconsistencies. Neither of them were All-County in sports, or valedictorians, but they have done well in life so far, and they have made us proud. Each stage of our children's lives has been a joy. Congratulations to Adam and Amy from your happy parents and your sister Katie. May God continue to bless our family. I am so grateful to Him.

May - 2005

PRISON NEWS

Do you know someone in prison? Until I started prison ministry in 1990, I think I only knew two people personally who had gone to prison. Today, one out of a hundred Americans is in prison! More and more people are coming to me and asking how to get in touch with their son/nephew/brother who is in prison. Last month I was at a women's prison and one of the ladies said she was from Holmes County. When I asked where, she said, "Benton." My town! I didn't know her personally, but I remember seeing her at a rental home here in town.

The next week I was at an Ohio prison and ate lunch with the prisoners. At my table of four were three other men from Holmes County! Prisoners are not just out there or from the big cities anymore. Our neighbors and acquaintances (and family members) are there. As our culture gets farther from God, as morality slides downward, and as the laws get stricter and more inconsistent, more and more people will go to prison. It's the only solution our government has for crime right now.

I believe that no matter what the circumstances, each person is responsible for his own actions. But in our modern culture, I'm never sure if that person in the prison chapel is there because of murder, robbery or... Bible reading! Note the following paragraph from Elton Yutzy's article in a Columbus newspaper in May 2005:

> At a school in Tennessee, some ten-year-olds were reading the Bible on the school playground during recess. A parent came by and observed them reading the Bible and reported it to the principle. The principal immediately went out and told them they cannot read the Bible on the playground (even during recess) while school is in session. That same week in Columbus, OH, as students were raping a mentally challenged girl in the auditorium, the principal walked by, noticed what was happening, and did nothing about it.

Then Yutzy asks the rhetorical question: "I wonder what she would have done if she had observed some students reading the Bible in the auditorium during school hours?"

She has been fired and is now having a hearing about the firing. She wants it to be a public hearing so the public can hear what is going on in our schools, but the school board wants it private. I guess they don't want the public to know what goes on in our public schools.

"Righteousness exalts a nation, but sin is a reproach to any people." (Proverbs 14:34)

My take on this is that the more we distance ourselves from God and His laws, the more confused we will be. We don't seem to know right from wrong. Preacher Roy Putnam said, "When you turn away from God, you don't turn to nothing; you turn to anything."

If you are one of those who personally know someone in prison, remember the words of Jesus, "I was in prison and you came to visit me" (Matthew 25:36).

June - 2005

THE POWER OF GOD'S WORD

A prisoner at Somerset Correctional told me his story:

He broke into an apartment and as he started up the stairs to rob the place, a man came to the top of the stairs and said firmly, "Acts 2:38!" The robber stopped in his tracks and the man yelled again, "Acts 2:38!" The robber turned around and ran out the door he had just broken down and he ran right into the arms of two policemen, who had heard breaking glass and came to check it out.

When the apartment dweller was asked how he scared off the robber, he explained that there is power in God's word and he proclaimed Acts 2:38, ("Repent and be baptized, every one of you in the name of Jesus Christ...") At the police station, my prisoner friend was asked why he ran and he said, "Hey, when he yelled the warning that he had an ax and two .38s, I knew I was no match for him!"

WHAT ARE WE DOING?

On July 1, we started out by celebrating my parents 60th wedding anniversary. My parents are not perfect, but one thing they did perfectly—they stayed together for sixty years! My dad is the kind of man who would be like the Arkansas farmer who was leaning on the fence after feeding the hogs. His wife was beside him, and she said, "It's our 50th anniversary. We ought to do something special. Let's kill one of the hogs." He replied, "Why punish a pig for something that happened fifty years ago?"

August - 2005

ARE YOU AFRAID TO DIE?

Our trip to Pakistan was canceled. I had been invited to go with a team to a pastor's conference and crusade in the city of Karachi. Every time I mentioned that I was going there, the reaction was always the same: "Pakistan? Are you crazy?" I don't think I'm crazy, but the more I learned about the political climate and the attitudes of Pakistanis toward Americans, and specifically Christian Americans, the more I started to doubt my sanity. I started to realize that this may not be a warm fuzzy mission trip, but a dangerous invasion into enemy territory. When I heard, "Don't go," I was reminded of all the other times in my life when I was warned to not take a chance: "Don't go to college." "Don't build silos." "Don't go to Costa Rica." "Don't buy a motorcycle." "Don't cross the road."

Well-meaning and cautious friends offered all these warnings to me, and if I would have listened to their counsel, I would be sitting in some office with a seat belt, a hard hat, and an oxygen mask, safely doing my work. Instead, I went to college, built silos, went to Costa Rica, bought a motorcycle, crashed several times (See? We told you...) and I have crossed a bunch of roads. I have the scars, broken bones, failures, and successes to prove it. Life is a risk.

A good friend of mine who had been to Pakistan called his friend, a high government official in Pakistan, who then called me. He said it would dangerous for us to come, and he could help us if we wouldn't be coming to a Christian event, but his hands were tied because of the anti-Christian sentiment in Pakistan. His recommendation: Don't come.

Now what? This was not CNN or well-meaning, cautious friends; this was an insider. Where does a Christian draw the line between courage and stupidity; between cowardice and being an idiot? Paul said, "What do you mean by weeping? For I am ready not only to be bound, but also to die at Jerusalem for the name of the Lord Jesus" (Acts 21:13 NKJV). On the other hand, Proverbs says, "A prudent man foresees evil and hides himself; The simple pass on and are punished" (Proverbs 22:3 NKJV). I was not taking this lightly, but I made my decision. I will do whatever the team leader decides. (I was told, for future security reasons, not to mention names.) But each night of the week before the trip, as I sat on the porch of the beautiful home the Lord gave me, I was thinking to myself, "I wonder if I'll ever see this again. Will I come back?"

On August 1, the team leader called and said, "We've made our decision." I said with confidence, "I'll do whatever you decide." He said, "We've called it off." I said, "I am at peace with that decision," but what I really wanted to say was,

"Praise the Lord! My chances of survival have just taken a significant rise!"

I am glad I didn't back down, but I am even "gladder" that we didn't go. But it has made me think how easy we have it here in the U.S. Our brethren in other countries are dying for their faith, but many of us here are just dying. The week I was supposed to be in Pakistan, I was recording a new CD that will be called, *Almost Bluegrass*. As I recorded, "Are You Afraid To Die," that old Louvin Brothers song took on new meaning.

September - 2005

A LETTER FROM PRISON

I want to thank you and your wife for coming to Cambridge Springs. I just returned to my unit and couldn't stop talking about the chapel service. I walked out of church with a great feeling. Thank you for that. I know God brought me here to bring me closer to Himself. Before I came here I had never been arrested, but I sure was full of sin. I didn't go to church and I didn't read my Bible. I was aimlessly coasting through life, looking for what would make me happy next. Since being here, I have found what keeps me happy all the time: my relationship with God. Anyhow, I wanted to thank you for coming here and sharing your testimony and talents. It really touched my heart...

–HEATHER

It's an exaggeration to say, "Ninety percent of prison ministry is showing up," but it contains more than a grain of truth.

Proverbs 25 says, "Like cold water to a weary soul is good news from a distant land." When you're in prison, anyone from the outside is from that distant land, and we bring cold fresh water (good news). And like this lady says, she didn't care to hear the good news until she was in prison.

FRIENDS OF COMMON GROUND MINISTRIES TOUR?

We are taking a tour! Join me on a singing tour to Branson, MO, Hot Springs, AR, and Nashville, TN! I have been invited to sing several songs on The Little Opry in Branson with Rich Langston, and then go on to the Music Mountain Jamboree in Hot Springs, AR, with Harvey Perdue. We are teaming up with Pioneer Trails and we have room for fifty people to go along! We leave on Thursday, November 17, visit the Arch in St. Louis, then on to Branson and Hot Springs for Friday and Saturday nights. On Sunday we will attend the Cowboy Church of Hot Springs where Harvey Perdue is pastor. On Monday the 21st we head for Nashville where I am invited to sing with Joanne Cash (Johnny's sister) and George Hamilton IV (Abilene), and possibly others.

NOTICE: Due to the rising costs of postage, paper, and gas, we have been forced to double the cost of your subscription to the CGM Newsletter.

However, because your cost is currently $0.00, and because 2 x $0.00 = $0.00... you still owe us absolutely nothing! But, because of your generosity over the years, we are able to meet the rising costs of going to prisons and churches in Ohio and across the US, as well as mission trips overseas. Thank you!

October - 2005

WILMA

I am writing this letter from a hotel room in Tampa, FL, while Hurricane Wilma is screaming outside. I was scheduled to come to Sarasota on October 22 to be a part of Steve Wingfield's Anniversary Celebration Banquet. Several days before departure I got the word that a good friend from Sarasota, Bert Miller, had died and the funeral was the 21st, so I changed my ticket (no small feat) and came a day early to help honor and celebrate the life of a solid, steady Christian man, and to mourn with the family.

The funeral was a victory celebration, the Wingfield banquet was fun and challenging, and every aspect of the trip went well until I confirmed my flight home and found that everybody was talking about Wilma. I wasn't sure I knew her, but the way people talked, she must be big and powerful. (Just kidding—I knew who she was.) Anyway, my morning flight was canceled and I'm scheduled to try again this afternoon. The eye of the storm is further south and it may be calm here by 2:00 pm.

Last month I mentioned the song, "Are You Afraid To Die" that I recorded, because it took on new meaning to me due to circumstances in my life. As I hear the wind outside and see the palm trees waving back and forth, 1 am reminded of another song on the recording *Almost Bluegrass,* a song entitled, "Troublesome Waters." The theme of that song is that God will not necessarily keep us away from storms, but He will guide our boat until we safely land on shore, and we don't have to be afraid.

Troublesome waters, much blacker than night
Are hiding from view the harbor's bright lights
I cried to my Savior, have mercy on me.

Then gently I'm feeling the touch of His hand,
Guiding my boat back safely to land.
Leading the way to heaven's bright shore;
Troublesome waters I'm fearing no more.

Storms in life are inevitable, but God has promised us shelter. "For you have been a shelter for me, A strong tower from the enemy..." (Psalms 61:3). God also assures us in Isaiah 25:4, "You have been... a refuge from the storm."

If you are reading this, you will know that I made it through the storm. His hand will guide us if we look to Him. 9/11, the tsunami, and Katrina have taught us that in this world there is no security. He is our shelter in the storm. He is our security. We can trust Him.

November - 2005

MERRY CHRISTMAS!

This is one of the busiest times of the year for me. But, I'm not complaining... I love this time of year. The banquets (sixteen of 'em) are not only a blast, but for about an hour I have the privilege of being an insider in many businesses, churches, and families as I sit at the table with the owners and head honchos. I eat real good this time of year and 90 percent of the banquets are right here at home, so I don't have to travel very far.

My style of ministry—singing fun, non-spiritual songs, and then transforming into a message about the real meaning of life (Christ)—is so easy at Christmas time. No matter how far off the path I get with crazy songs and funny stories, all I have to do is sing a familiar Christmas carol and the transition is made. Most of the time, everyone joins in the singing, usually with a feeling of good cheer and a touch of nostalgia, and I simply remind the folks of what they have just sung and the subject is now, Jesus.

HAPPY HOLIDAYS?

Many businesses will now wish you Happy Holidays instead of "Merry Christmas." When pastor Elton Yutzy received the bill at Bob Evans last Sunday, it had "Happy Holidays" written on it. He decided to not be silent. He said to the waitress, "Ma'am, if you want a big tip, you'd better take that 'Happy Holidays' off and write 'Merry Christmas.' " She took it back and ran another tab off the register that read, "Merry Christmas" in bright red. (Big tip.) When Elton paid the bill, he told the cashier what he had done. She smiled a sad smile and said she agreed, but if she wants to keep her job, she has to say what they tell her to say.

I agree with Elton that it's not so much the merchants refusing to say "Merry Christmas," but it's the spirit behind it. We stood by and said nothing as they took prayer, Bible reading, and the Ten Commandments out of our schools; the nativity scene from public places; "in Jesus' name" from any public prayer. They're trying to remove "under God" from the pledge of allegiance, and "In God we trust" from our currency. Now stores are forbidding their employees from saying, "Merry Christmas." Why? I guess because it's "religious."

I realize that just having these words on our money and in certain documents doesn't mean that our government or businesses actually trust God, but to forbid employees from saying the traditional Christmas greeting at Christmas time shows that the enemy is serious about wiping out any remembrance of when our nation acknowledged God as the Supreme Being. I have been inspired by Elton's example. I am going to say something when a merchant wishes me "Happy Holidays." I may even return merchandise and inform the manager that I would rather shop at a store that doesn't bow to the whims of a few vocal offended non-religious activists. I love Christmas (and I love Christ) and I want to hear that traditional greeting: MERRY CHRISTMAS!

December - 2005

LEARN MORE ABOUT
COMMON GROUND MINISTRIES:

www.johnschmid.org

P.O. Box 178, Berlin, Ohio 44610

johnschmid89@gmail.com